Who Wrote
the Gospels?

D0879189

Pereset Press Books by Gary Greenberg

The Moses Mystery: *The Egyptian Origins of the Jewish People*

King David Versus Israel: *How a Hebrew Tyrant Hated by the Israelites Became a Biblical Hero*

Also by Gary Greenberg

101 Myths of the Bible: *How Ancient Scribes Invented Biblical History*

The Judas Brief: *Who Really Killed Jesus?*

Manetho: *A Study in Egyptian Chronology*

Who Wrote the Gospels?

Why New Testament Scholars Challenge Church Traditions

Gary Greenberg

PERE/ET PRE//
New York, NY

Copyright © 2011 by Gary Greenberg

Cover and internal design by JoAnne Chernow

All rights reserved. No part of this book may be reproduced in any form or by any electronic or mechanical means including information storage and retrieval systems— except in the case of brief quotations embodied in critical articles or reviews—without permission in writing from its publisher, Pereset Press, or from the copyright holder.

A Pereset Press book.

All inquiries should be addressed to
Pereset Press
P.O. Box 25
New York, NY 10008

Contact info@peresetpress.com

First published as a paperback in 2011.

Greenberg, Gary
Who Wrote the Gospels?
Why New Testament Scholars Challenge Church Traditions
ISBN: 978-0-9814966-3-4
1. Bible. -- N.T. -- Criticism, Textual.
2. Bible. -- N.T. -- Gospels -- Criticism, interpretation, etc.
3. Christianity -- Controversial literature.
4. Synoptic problem.
5. Bible. -- N.T. -- John -- Criticism, interpretation, etc.

Library of Congress Control Number: 2011906280

Unless otherwise indicated, all biblical quotations are taken from the New Revised Standard Version.

Contents

Tables

Who Wrote the Gospels?

CHAPTER 1

The Problem of Gospel Authorship

*A*sking who wrote the four canonical Gospels may seem like an odd question. According to Church tradition the four authors were Matthew, Mark, Luke and John. This tradition further holds that Matthew and John were two of the Twelve Apostles, Mark was a secretary to the Apostle Peter and Luke was a companion of the Apostle Paul. All in all this Church tradition boasts quite a stellar cast of writers with a good claim to a reasonable amount of historical credibility, authors who were either eyewitnesses or intimate with eyewitnesses to the mission of Jesus and its aftermath. Most New Testament historians, however, question these identifications, arguing on the basis of historical evidence and logical assumptions arising from literary analysis of the texts that none of the four authors were intimates of either Jesus or of the Apostles.[1]

In this book we will look at a number of the reasons why New Testament historians reject the Church traditions about the Gospel authors. As we will see below, the authors of each of the Gospels were anonymous and for the first couple of centuries of Christianity the identities of the authors were a mystery. It is only towards the end of the second century that Christian writers began to assign the traditional names to the authors and the evidence for such determinations was shaky at best. As early Christian scholars began to repeat the speculations of other Christian scholars the guesses became traditions and the traditions became accepted as fact.

While the sparseness of the evidence prevents us from connecting the Gospel authors with any particular historical individuals, there is enough evidence such that we can reject the idea that the traditional identifications carry any historical weight. Matthew, Mark, Luke and John did not write the Gospels, at least not the Matthew, Mark, Luke and John traditionally associated with the Gospels. Despite this conclusion, the traditional identities are so tightly woven into our cultural context and into all of our literature that it is nearly impossible to talk intelligently about the Gospels without using the names of the traditional authors. So for purposes of convenience, I will frequently refer to the authors as Matthew, Mark, Luke or John, or to the Gospels associated with those names. That should not be taken to mean that I accept those names as the proper identities. It is just a simple convention to avoid convoluted phrasing to refer to the authors or to the Gospels associated with those names.

In addition to the identity of a Gospel author, we are also concerned with other questions related to authorship. A major concern is the matter of sources. Did the author create his own text or did he copy large parts of his work from someone else, tinkering around the edges for literary or theological reasons and perhaps rearranging the material for similar reasons? We also want to know if the Gospels as we have them are the Gospels as they were written. Did scribes along the way make significant changes to the text, adding to, deleting from, or rearranging the material as preserved in the copy the scribe worked from, and were those changes eventually incorporated into the Gospels as if they were part of the original Gospel text?

In scholarly circles almost all modern New Testament scholars believe that Mark was the first Gospel to be written and that the authors of both Matthew and Luke copied most of Mark into their own manuscripts, occasionally modifying or rearranging Mark's work for their own editorial purposes. Almost all such scholars also believe that Matthew and Luke, writing independently of each other, both copied another large amount of material from a yet-to-be-discovered written source that scholars nicknamed "Q," from the German word *quelle*, meaning source. These two sources make up the bulk of Matthew and Luke. In Chapter Two we will look at some of the evidence that explains why scholars believe Matthew and Luke copied so much from Mark and Q.

While scholars are quite confident about Matthew and Luke copying from Mark, they are deeply divided over the question of whether the author of John relied in any significant way on the other three Gospels. While they almost all believe that John had some written sources for some of his work, they are probably split down the middle as to whether the author of John knew any of the other Gospels, especially Mark. On a separate note, most Johannine scholars believe that John is not the work of a single author. While they credit the vast bulk of his Gospel to an original author, they believe several portions of John were added at a later time, mostly by someone they refer to as the Redactor, believed to have been a devoted follower of the author. In Chapter Three we will look at some of the evidence that divides scholars over the matter of John's use of the other Gospels. We'll also look at some of the evidence for the use of earlier written sources as well as the idea that a Redactor made changes to John's Gospel. We will also look at evidence that John and Luke shared a common Passion source that may not have been known to Mark.

In Chapter Four I will set forth my own arguments in support of the idea that John made use of a written source for his Passion account and made changes to his source material. We will also look at reasons to believe Luke also had access to a similar source. We will also explore the question of whether or not Mark knew this written source and made his own modifications.

A key problem in Gospel studies (and New Testament studies in general) is that we have no original copies of any book in the New Testament. Our earliest evidence for any textual content in the Christian scriptures dates only to the first half of the second century (a more precise date is difficult to determine) and consists of just a couple of verses from the Gospel of John.[2] For the rest of the second century we have only a handful of Gospel fragments.[3] All-in-all, however, from the second to seventeenth centuries, we have over 3000 handwritten Greek manuscripts that contain whole or partial copies of the New Testament.[4] We also have over 2200 lectionaries containing handwritten portions of the New Testament in Greek.[5] In addition we have some ancient copies of early handwritten manuscripts that translate Greek copies of the New Testament into other languages, including Old Latin, Old Syriac, and Coptic.[6] We don't begin to see complete written copies of any of the Gospels until the fourth century.[7]

The problem we face is that with the exception of a handful of small fragments no two of those manuscripts are identical in the overlapping portions.[8] The variations number in the hundreds of thousands, more than all of the words in the New Testament.[9] To be sure, the vast majority of differences can be traced to copying errors and when these are accounted for we can reconstruct most of the underlying text that lay behind these many copies. But in several instances we can see that scribes made significant alterations to the text they were copying from. We know this because we have copies of manuscripts which contain corresponding verses that differ in significant ways and these variations sometimes raise theological questions about early Christian beliefs. The existence of such variants was well known even in ancient times and many of the early church fathers commented on the differences in the texts and made judgment calls about what they believed to be most reliable readings. But they didn't always agree with each other.

In Chapter Five we will look at how our modern Gospel text developed and some of the ways New Testament scholars deal with the conflicting manuscripts and try to determine which version of a textual passage most likely comes closest to the original Gospel text. We will see that in the first few centuries of Christianity scribes made a large number of alterations and changes to the Gospel texts, with many such changes having significant theological impacts. We will look at such issues as added or altered endings to the Gospels, new stories being added to the Gospels, text being changed or modified, and the impact of heresies on the transmission of the Gospel text. We will also see why New Testament historians reject the version of the New Testament known as the Textus Receptus, which underlies the King James Version of the bible, and why they propose an alternative textual reconstruction of the original Greek text of the New Testament.

THE ANONYMOUS NATURE OF THE GOSPEL AUTHORS

All four Gospels were originally written anonymously, with no identification of the author.[10] Although Church tradition says that Matthew and

John were among the Twelve Disciples of Jesus, neither of the two Gospels attributed to them makes such a claim. The Gospel of Matthew, for example, refers to the Apostle Matthew in the third person, with no indication that author and Apostle are one and the same (Matt 9:9, 10:3). John 21:24 claims as a source for the Gospel someone known as the "Beloved Disciple" but does not say who this person was. Elsewhere in the text we find several references to the acts of the Beloved Disciple but nowhere does the author of the Gospel of John give any hint that he and the Beloved Disciple are one and the same person (see John 13:23, 19:26, 20:2).

While the Gospel of John clearly distinguishes between Peter and the Beloved Disciple (John 21:20), and obviously rejects any connection between Judas Iscariot and the Beloved Disciple, it does not give us any direct evidence as to which of the Apostles or other disciples of Jesus we can identify with this revered individual.

If any of the Twelve Apostles or one of their close associates had written a report about the activities of Jesus one would expect such a work to have become an instant classic in Christian circles, widely copied, distributed, and cited, and the author frequently mentioned by name by other Christian writers. Yet, on the basis of writings from the first four centuries of Christianity, it appears that as late as the last years of the second century, almost two centuries after the death of Jesus, the early Christian scholars could only guess at who wrote the four canonical Gospels. Only towards the end of the second century do we begin to see Christian authors associate the canonical Gospels with the traditional authors. But those who made these identifications either utilized unreliable sources or simply asserted that the identification was correct without any evidence to support the allegation. Prior to that time Christian writers appear to have thought of these four Gospels generically as the "memoirs" of the Apostles,[11] without any specific attribution, and identified them by characteristics of the text, such as "the Gospels with the genealogies."[12]

Moreover, in the first few centuries of Christianity these weren't the only Gospels floating around. We have indications of over thirty different Gospels circulating, many falsely attributed to either Apostles or to other persons mentioned in the Gospels.[13] Among the most important of these other Gospels, primarily due to their priority, were the Gospel of Peter and the Gospel of Thomas, which may have been written contemporaneously with some of the canonical Gospels. The other non-canonical Gospels were probably written a century or more after the canonical Gospels.

The Gospel of Peter had been widely circulated in Syria and apparently read as scripture in some churches.[14] During the second century Christians were openly debating its authenticity.[15] At about the end of the second century Bishop Serapion of Antioch barred its use in churches, apparently because it came to be seen as containing heretical claims about Jesus.[16] The Gospel of Thomas may have been highly popular in Gnostic Christian circles and may have been widely distributed in Christian communities. Most New Testament historians would date the authorship of these two texts to the early years of the second century or perhaps the last years of the first century,[17] with a few scholars arguing that one or the other may have been written prior to the four canonical Gospels.[18]

The forgery of Gospels and letters and other writings in the name of Apostles and other figures from the time of Jesus appears to have been something of a cottage industry in Christian circles during the first few centuries. A handful of falsified documents may have even made their way into the New Testament. The large majority of New Testament historians, for example, only accept seven of the thirteen letters attributed to Paul as coming from his hand or having been written during his lifetime.[19] The letters of Paul that scholars acknowledge as authentic include 1 Thessalonians, Galatians, Philemon, Philippians, 1 and 2 Corinthians, and Romans.[20] These seven Pauline letters appear to be the earliest Christian writings that we know of, generally dating to the early 50s.[21] A majority would also reject the claim that the letters attributed to Peter, James, and Jude came from their hand.[22]

THE EVIDENCE FOR MATTHEW AND MARK

The identification in Christian tradition of Matthew and Mark as the authors of the respective Gospels attributed to them seems to derive from an unreliable claim from an early second century Christian writer named Papias. Our evidence about his attribution comes from the fourth century Church historian Eusebius.[23] While Eusebius cites Papias's testimony favorably with respect to the Gospel origins, he appears to have little regard for the man's intelligence, calling him a person "of very limited understanding."[24]

According to Eusebius, who claims to have copies of this earlier Christian's writings, Papias set out to collect the traditions about the teachings of the Apostles. He himself had never met any of the Apostles[25] and he relied on oral traditions from the elders of his day for information,[26] suggesting that these various elders were unaware of any specific writings attributed to the Apostles who knew Jesus. He mentions the existence of Christian writings but does not consider them as reliable as what the elders had to say about oral traditions.[27] This strongly suggests that these other known Christian writings were not attributed to the apostolic circle that knew Jesus.

Papias, says Eusebius, wrote that one of the elders told him about two texts, one written by someone named Mark, who was believed to have been "the interpreter of" the apostle Peter, and the other written by the Apostle Matthew. (The use of the word "interpreter" is odd and ambiguous and scholars aren't sure as to what it means.) Eusebius quotes him, regarding this Mark document, as follows.

> Mark having become the interpreter of Peter, wrote down accurately, though not in order, whatsoever he remembered of the things said or done by Christ. For he neither heard the Lord nor followed him, but afterward, as I said, he followed Peter, who adapted his teaching to the needs of his hearers, but with no intention of giving a connected account of the Lord's discourses, so that Mark committed no error while he thus wrote some things as he remembered them. For he was careful of one thing, not to omit any of the things which he had heard, and not to state any of them falsely.[28]

Eusebius then says that Papias added the following remark about Matthew.

> So then Matthew wrote the oracles in the Hebrew language, and every one interpreted them as he was able.[29]

These two quotes comprise all of Papias' known commentary on the alleged origins of the Gospels of Mark and Matthew. A major difficulty with Papias' description of Mark's Gospel is that he describes it as "not in order," referring apparently to the sequence of events in Jesus' life, when in fact Mark's Gospel is clearly presented in an orderly fashion. It seems unlikely that someone who had read the actual Gospel of Mark would think of it as disorderly.

Closely related to the question of what text Papias referred to is the fact (noted previously) that there was probably in wide circulation at that time a Gospel of Peter. Since Papias claims that this Mark received his information from Peter, it is possible that the text the elder referred to was not canonical Mark but rather the Gospel of Peter. Without any references to the content there is no way to know whether this alleged Gospel authored by a Mark is canonical Mark, the Gospel of Peter, or some other document altogether. And, even if it is canonical Mark, we have no way to know if the author actually was an associate of Peter or just rumored to be a colleague.

Papias' attribution of a Gospel to Matthew presents another difficult problem, the claim that Matthew wrote his text in Hebrew or Aramaic. It is overwhelmingly accepted among New Testament historians that the author of the Gospel of Matthew wrote in Greek and that the text bears no indicia of having been translated into Greek from Aramaic.[30] As Bart Ehrman observes, "If our Matthew was a Greek translation of a Hebrew original it would be impossible to explain the verbatim agreement of Matthew with Mark in the Greek itself.[31] So, whatever text Papias is talking about, it is not the Gospel of Matthew as we now know it.

While it might be argued that Papias actually refers to an Aramaic translation of the Greek version of the Gospel of Matthew, and evidence indicates that Aramaic translations existed at some point in time (but almost certainly not before the second century), that seems unlikely since it should have been known that the text was originally written in Greek and translated into Aramaic, rather than the other way around. As with his references to a work by Mark, here, too, there is no citation to any of the content of the written work so that it may be compared to what we now know as the Gospel of Matthew.

In sum, then, at the beginning of the second century we have an unidentified source giving Papias an oral tradition alleging that there were Gospels written by a Matthew and a Mark. But Papias never saw these written works, the description of their contents is inconsistent with what we know about the nature of the canonical Gospels, and Eusebius considers Papias to be something of a dunce. Despite these historical difficulties, this early Christian writer seems to be responsible for a trend developing in the late second century and continuing into the early third century to identify the authors of two of the canonical Gospels as Matthew and Mark, and to further identify Matthew as one of the Twelve Apostles and Mark as the secretary to Peter.

In the late second century, the Christian writer Irenaeus, repeats the claims made by Papias, that Matthew wrote his Gospel in the dialect used by the Hebrews and that Mark, the disciple and "interpreter" of Peter, wrote the other Gospel.[32] But he doesn't tell us where he got this information from. His reference to Matthew being written in the Hebrew dialect and to Mark being the "interpreter" of Peter, that odd word also used by Papias, indicates that Irenaeus used Papias as his source.

Shortly thereafter, in the early third century, Origen, one of the most learned and respected of ancient Christian writers, says that Matthew wrote his Gospel in Aramaic (the language used by Hebrews in the time of Jesus) and it was published for believers of Jewish origin.[33] He also identified a Mark, Luke and John as the authors of a Gospel. But, as with Irenaeus, he doesn't say where he got this information from. He does, however, indicate that in his own time it was the traditional view and he accepted it, which suggests that he was unaware of any direct documentation for this tradition.[34] He also adds the claim that this Mark was the one mentioned in Peter's second epistle as being his son, which claim seems inconsistent with Papias's tradition about just being a secretary to Peter.[35]

This is the state of the evidence in the early third century for associating the Gospel of Matthew with the Apostle Matthew and the Gospel of Mark with an associate of the Apostle Peter. The evidence suggests that an undocumented oral tradition tracing to Papias and his contemporaries in a particular community became Christian dogma and with each subsequent mention of the claim by a Christian writer its authenticity became reinforced. The problem is that the validity of the claims by Papias, Irenaeus and Origen are historically questionable.

LUKE

The author of Luke specifically says that at the time he began his effort many others had already set down orderly accounts of what had been "handed on to us by those who from the beginning were eyewitnesses and servants of the word" (Luke 1:2). But he makes no particular claim that any of the Apostles had written a Gospel. In fact, his language suggests that the written sources he has came from persons other than the original witnesses and that these sources relied on oral traditions that may have been handed up by people who may have been eyewitnesses. If he did know of any writings by an Apostle, why wouldn't he specifically mention that source in order to add to his own credibility?

Luke 1:3–4 asserts that the Evangelist decided to investigate matters and prepare an orderly account for someone named Theophilus, so that he may know the truth. Who this Theophilus was, we don't know. His name may have been a metaphor for the Christian movement or the Christian reader of his text.[36] Luke doesn't name his sources nor tell us when he is citing a source. Tradition holds that Luke was a companion to Paul but the author of Luke makes no such claim and never says that he got any particular information from Paul.

Despite the lack of any noted association with Paul, the New Testament Acts of the Apostles, almost universally accepted as written by the author of the Gospel of Luke, includes some passages that led early Christians to believe that the author was a traveling companion of Paul. At several points in Acts the author uses the term "we" when talking about some activities of Paul.[37]

This use of "we" has led to the idea that Luke was with Paul at the time these events occurred and was writing a first-hand account of what took place. In 2 Tim 4:11, one of the disputed letters attributed to Paul, the author, allegedly Paul, says that "Only Luke is with me." In Col 4:14, another disputed letter attributed to Paul, the author identifies Luke as "the beloved physician." This led to the tradition that the author of Acts was Luke, the beloved physician who was with Paul.

On the other hand, the "we" passages may simply reflect the author's verbatim quotes from one of the sources he refers to and from which he took the "we" passages. One problem that most New Testament historians have with the idea of Luke being a companion of Paul is that much of what the author of Acts says about Paul conflicts with what Paul himself says about the same matters as reflected in Paul's letters.[38] The author of Acts seems to have had no knowledge of Paul's letters or any intimate knowledge of Paul's works from personal observation.[39] He appears to have even misunderstood Paul's theology.[40]

If the author of Luke-Acts knew Paul it would seem that the acquaintance was casual at best. The author of Luke, therefore, would seem to be somewhat removed from the Apostolic circles that emerged after the death of Jesus. If he were a companion of Paul, the many errors he makes with respect to Paul's career and teaching suggest that he should be read cautiously at best with regard to his accounts of Jesus. If he were not a close companion of Paul, that should make us even more wary.

To this we should add that Paul gives no indication that he himself had any personal knowledge of Jesus' life prior to the crucifixion. One can search his letters and find almost nothing about Jesus prior to his death. Paul may therefore be an unreliable source about Jesus' life and if Luke relied on Paul for the life of Jesus he would only have been receiving second- or third-hand information at best.

JOHN

As noted above, John 21:24 suggests that the Beloved Disciple was the source of the Gospel text but that the Gospel does not identify who the Beloved Disciple was. His identity is one of those interesting issues that Johannine scholars like to kick about.

The first evidence we have connecting the authorship of John with the Apostle John appears in the late second century, from the aforementioned Christian writer Irenaeus. In the passage in which he seems to rely on Papias for the claim that Matthew and Mark wrote the respective Gospels attributed to them (see above), he also makes the claim that the Beloved Disciple was named John, but he doesn't say how he knows this.[41] Nor does he quite say that this disciple was the Apostle John, although it would be hard to imagine that Irenaeus did not believe this to be the case. Nevertheless, by the fourth century this identification had become widely accepted among Christians.[42] As Origen said, it was the tradition in his time (third century) and he accepted it.

In considering the possibility that the Apostle John may have been the Beloved Disciple, we should note that the Gospel of John never refers to the Apostle John by name. Some might argue that the author didn't need to mention that Apostle's name since he referred to him as the Beloved Disciple. There is reason to reject that argument. In the Synoptic Gospels the Apostle John is identified as one of the sons of Zebedee. In John 21:2 the evangelist makes a casual offhand remark to the presence of the "sons of Zebedee" and some other disciples without any hint that one of the sons of Zebedee (i.e., John) was the Beloved Disciple.

The reference in John 21:24 to the Beloved Disciple being the source of the Gospel's information seems to speak of the Beloved Disciple in the third person, suggesting that there is a distinction between the author of John 21:24 and the Beloved Disciple. In Johannine studies it is commonly accepted that the author of John 21, the final chapter in that Gospel, is not the author of the preceding chapters.[43] We'll discuss this point further in Chapters Three and Five.

WHEN WERE THE GOSPELS WRITTEN?

If we can't be sure who wrote the Gospels, it would be helpful to know when they were written. Were the authors personally familiar with the events or did they have to rely on earlier sources for their information? If the latter, then how good were these sources? Were they written close in time to the events in question, before several competing traditions and theologies developed, or on a later occasion, after a wide range of conflicting views emerged? Once the link to the traditional identity of the authors is broken, these questions become more difficult to resolve. The best evidence would be written copies of some portion of each of the Gospels that could be dated or citations to the Gospels by some author whose writing can be dated. Extant evidence of this sort, however, leaves a very wide range of possible dates for authorship.

As mentioned above our earliest written evidence for the Gospels is a tiny fragment of John dating to the early half of the second century. This suggests the latest possible date for that writing of that Gospel. We don't begin to see evidence for the existence of the other Gospels until about the last quarter of the second century and early third century. Our earliest complete Gospels date to the fourth century.[44] While we don't have evidence associating the Gospels with particular authors until about the end of the second century, references in the Patristic literature suggest that the texts themselves were in circulation earlier than that point. How much earlier is the problem to be resolved?

In establishing a latest possible date, one criterion used by many scholars is the absence of any reference to the great Jewish revolt of Bar Kokhba at about 132 C.E. and the devastating impact on the Jews when the Romans eventually put down the rebellion and barred the Jews from Jerusalem, their holy city. Given the hostility of Christians towards Jews who didn't accept Jesus, it seems highly unlikely that if Gospel authors knew about the rebellion they would have missed the opportunity to mention the result as a punishment of the Jews by God. The absence of such references suggests to many scholars that the Gospels were almost certainly written before this revolt.

As to the earliest likely date scholars have tried to use certain themes and literary relationships to narrow the time frame. For Matthew, Mark and Luke, one of the chief criteria for dating the Gospels involves the issue of whether the Gospels contain references to the Roman destruction of the Jewish Temple in 70 C.E. Mark 13:2 records a prophecy by Jesus, to wit, "Do you see these great buildings? Not one stone will be left here upon another; all will be thrown down." A variation of this prophecy also appears in Matt 24:2 and Luke 21:6. In addition, Matt 22:7 has Jesus say, "The king was enraged. He sent his troops, destroyed those murderers, and burned their city." In Luke 19:43 Jesus says, "Indeed, the days will come upon you, when your enemies will set up ramparts around you and surround you, and hem you in on every side."

These passages suggest to most New Testament historians that these three Gospels were probably written during or after the destruction of the Temple. But some scholars dispute these interpretations and argue that if the Gospels were written after the destruction of the Temple, the authors would have made more explicit reference to the destruction. This latter group argues for a pre-70 c.e. date for all of the Gospels. Raymond Brown, one of the most respected Christian scholars, however, has observed that while there are occasional attempts to move the Gospel dates earlier none of the proposals have gained much of a scholarly following.[45] For some time those who connected Mark to the Jewish revolt against Rome were unsure if he wrote during the revolt or after the Temple's fall. Brown observes that there is a growing tendency to date Mark after 70.[46] As to Matthew and Luke, the overwhelming majority of scholars accept that Matt 22:7 and Luke 19:43 refer to the destruction of the Temple and tend to date Matthew and Luke from around 75 to 85.

Another criterion proposed by scholars for dating the Gospels focuses on the emphasis in the Gospels on the conflict between the Pharisees and the followers of Jesus, which suggests that the authors were writing in the post-Temple period when the Pharisees emerged as the dominant intellectual group among Jewish teachers and probably became the chief intellectual Jewish opposition to Christianity. In the time of Jesus there were other intellectual groups flourishing, including the Sadducees and the Essenes, both of which were wiped out during the Jewish revolt.

The Sadducees, had they survived, would have almost certainly opposed Christianity. Yet they are virtually invisible in the Gospels. Mark and Luke mention them just once, both describing the same minor incident. John doesn't mention them at all. Matthew has only a little additional material to add. We don't know enough about the Essenes to know how they would have reacted, but they were an ultra-orthodox Jewish group.

This lack of reference to the Sadducees is especially puzzling because the Sadducees were in control of the priesthood at the time Jesus was executed and if the Jewish Chief Priest urged Pilate to crucify Jesus, as all of the Gospels allege, that priest would have been a Sadducee. Although the author of Luke hides the fact in his Gospel that the Chief Priest and his circle were Sadducees, he lets slip in Acts 5:17 that the Chief priest and his allies belonged to that sect. If the Sadducees played such a major role in the prosecution of Jesus, as alleged in the Gospels, it is astounding that they are virtually ignored in the Gospel accounts. This absence of Sadducees in the Gospels, together with the emphasis on Pharisees as the opponents of Jesus, suggests that the Gospels were written after the Sadducees were gone from the scene and the Gospel authors had little idea who they actually were, a time frame suggesting a post-Temple period.

Dating the Gospel of John is more difficult because we don't have any clear chronological landmarks cited, such as the Temple destruction. The tendency is to argue that the enhanced nature of its theology and Christology and themes such as the expulsion of Christians from Jewish synagogues and the absence of any Jewish groups other than the Pharisees and priests suggest a post-70's environment. John, for example, at 1:1–3, is the only Gospel that explicitly identifies Jesus as a deity present at the Creation. Another question that scholars raise is whether or not the author of John knew the other Gospels. If he did then John would have to be dated after at least one of the other Gospels. The broad scholarly consensus is that John dates to about 90–110 C.E.

WHERE WERE THE GOSPELS WRITTEN?

Tradition places the authorship of Mark in Rome. Though possible, this view probably reflects the unreliable report of Papias concerning Mark as a secretary to Peter in Rome. A number of scholars have suggested Syria or the northern Transjordan.[47] A few scholars have suggested the Galilee but Raymond Brown, in his survey of the evidence, finds the argument unconvincing.[48]

As to Matthew, most scholars would probably place its origin in Antioch, in Syria, a city that had a very large Jewish population.[49] Luke's special interest in Paul's activities (as reflected in Acts) suggests that Luke probably addressed Pauline churches in Greece or Syria, where Paul conducted his missions.[50] As to John, the majority of scholars would probably place it in the Greek city of Ephesus, with some suggesting a Syrian locale.[51]

The broad scholarly consensus is that none of the Gospel authors wrote from Judea or Galilee or addressed themselves directly to persons from those areas.

SUMMARY

The evidence that the authors of the four canonical Gospels were Matthew, Mark, Luke and John, two of who were allegedly apostles of Jesus, one of whom was a secretary to Paul, and one of whom was a close companion of Paul, rests on extremely shaky and highly unreliable historical grounds. With the exception of Papias' untrustworthy account about a Matthew and a Mark, we have no indications prior to the end of the second century that Christians had identified the four canonical authors with specific individuals. Papias' evidence is almost worthless. It is based on an oral tradition that there existed written texts by a Matthew and a Mark. Papias never saw the texts and gives us no quotes from either text for comparison with the existing Gospels. Further, what he does tell us about the content is at odds with what we know about both texts. Finally, Papias' credibility as a reliable scholar is called into question by the one person who cites his account, the fourth century Christian historian Eusebius, who considered Papias rather dim-witted.

As to the identities of the authors of Luke and John there are no credible historical accounts that tell us how these two names came to be associated with the authorship of the two Gospels attributed to them. The "we" passages in Acts, which appear to be quotations from an external text, gave rise to the belief that the author was a companion to Paul, and there is a Luke mentioned as a companion of Paul in one of the disputed letters attributed to that Apostle.[52] Another disputed letter of Paul also refers to a Luke as "the beloved physician" but we don't know if that is the same Luke mentioned in the other letter.[53] And in one of the accepted letters of Paul there is a reference to a fellow-worker named Luke but, here to we don't know if this Luke is one and the same as the other Lukes mentioned.[54] However, the author of Luke-Acts doesn't seem to have any direct knowledge about Paul and his writings about Paul are frequently at odds with what Paul says in his own letters. The Gospel of John, in a passage of questionable authorship, cites an unidentified individual, the Beloved Disciple, as the author. Who this individual was is unclear but internal textual evidence suggests he was not the apostle John.

It is widely accepted among New Testament historians that the Gospels were originally written in Greek, from outside of Palestine, sometime between the years 65 and 110. Who wrote the Gospels remains an open question, but the evidence available shows that none of the authors were witnesses to what happened or had any direct connection to the apostolic circle of Jesus.

CHAPTER 2

The Synoptic Problem

Scholars refer to the Gospels of Matthew, Mark and Luke as the "Synoptic Gospels." This is because if you placed the three Gospels side by side you will see that there are a large number of stories that appear in all three Gospels. It is often the case that in these triplicate accounts that at least two, if not all three, of the Gospels share some of the same key words and phrases. It is also the case that in many instances at least two, if not all three, place the collection of stories in the same chronological sequence. Even where sequences vary in one Gospel or the other, we find frequent key word or phrase agreements within the stories.

To get an idea of the relationship between these three texts, consider these statistics. Mark has 661 verses, Matthew 1068, and Luke 1,149.[55] Of all the verses in Mark, 80 per cent have close parallels in Matthew and 65 per cent in Luke.[56] This means that approximately one-half of Matthew overlaps Mark and over one-third of Luke overlaps Mark. Scholars refer to those verses appearing in all three Gospels as the "Triple Tradition."[57]

In addition to the Triple Tradition of the Synoptic Gospels, we have what is known as the "Double Tradition."[58] This refers to a substantial amount of material that appears in both Matthew and Luke but which doesn't appear in Mark. As a general rule, most scholars believe that the Double Tradition derives from a lost source that they refer to as "Q." In most of these instances the material tends to feature sayings or teachings by Jesus. Again, we have a good deal of agreement as to language and some lesser degree of agreement on the order of the stories. While there is some debate about which verses do or do not belong in Q, Raymond Brown estimates that the range encompasses about 220–235 verses.[59] John S. Kloppenborg, one of the leading experts in this area, has determined that there are 106 textual units (as opposed to verses) that fall into this category and that 35, about a third, share a common sequential arrangement.[60] Approximately twenty percent of Matthew and Luke encompasses the Double Tradition.[61]

The frequent verbal and sequential agreement within both the Triple Tradition and the Double Tradition suggests to almost all New Testament scholars that there must be some sort of literary relationship among these texts.[62] Did all three share a common written source? Did one of the texts influence the other two? Did one of the authors have access to the other two texts? What literary relationship these Gospels have to each other is known as the "Synoptic Problem."

The almost universal view among scholars is that Mark was the first Gospel to be written and that Matthew and Luke both used Mark as a source.[63] As to the Double Tradition, the overwhelmingly dominant view is that Matthew and Luke wrote independently of each other, neither knowing the other's work, and both made use of a lost written source that scholars nicknamed "Q," from the German word *quelle* meaning "source."[64] Scholars refer to the idea that Matthew and Luke drew upon Mark and Q as the "Two-Source Theory."[65]

Mark Goodacre, a leading critic of the Q theory, notes the degree to which the Q theory has been accepted in scholarly circles. "This lost document has become an elementary resource for knowledge about the New Testament, a staple of introductory courses on Christian origins and indispensible for research into the historical Jesus."[66] Despite its widespread acceptance among scholars the Q theory is not without some challenge. The two leading schools of opposition adhere to either the Farrar Theory or the Griesbach Hypothesis.

The Farrar Theory, named after Austin Farrar, has its roots in British scholarly circles.[67] It accepts the principle of Markan priority but holds that Luke used both Mark and Matthew as a source. A key element of the Farrar theory is the problem of "Minor Agreements."[68] These are some of the rare instances in which Matthew and Luke agree against Mark and no good explanation for this disagreement exists. These occasionally include an odd word peculiar to Matthew which pops up in a parallel story in Luke.[69] If Luke used Matthew then there is no need to posit a Q document to account for the Double Tradition. The coincidences would stem from Luke's use of Matthew.

The Griesbach Hypothesis dates to 1789.[70] It argues for Matthean priority on the ground that from antiquity Matthew has always been thought of as the first Gospel.[71] The idea that Matthew was the first Gospel to be written goes back to at least Augustine in the fourth century.[72] In addition to Matthean priority the Griesbach Hypothesis holds that Luke used Matthew, and Mark used Matthew and Luke.[73] It claims that Mark originated primarily as a digest version of Matthew and Luke, based on those areas where the two Gospels agreed.[74] Brown argues that this thesis fails to come to grips with the fact that Mark omits the entire Double Tradition, where Matthew and Luke agree but the verses don't appear within Mark.[75]

Mainstream scholars acknowledge that the Two-Source Theory, that Matthew and Luke used Mark and Q, is not without some problems.[76] As a number of scholars have observed, there is no perfect solution to the Synoptic Problem and that all proposed theories have some defects. The Two-Source theory appears to most to be the one that seems to be the least problematic and provides the best explanation for the various agreements.[77]

If we subtract the Triple Tradition and the Double Tradition from Matthew and Luke that leaves about thirty percent of Matthew and about forty percent of Luke that is unique to each of the respective Gospels. Scholars refer to that unique portion of Matthew as "M" and the unique portion of Luke as "L." The vast bulk of M and L consists primarily of the two very different infancy narratives in the two Gospels. The idea that Matthew and Luke drew upon Mark, Q, M and L is known as the "Four-Source Theory."[78]

EVIDENCE OF SEQUENTIAL AGREEMENT IN THE TRIPLE TRADITION

In order to show how these three Gospels occasionally place the same set of stories in the same narrative order I set up a comparison between the first twelve stories in Mark and the order of those same stories in Matthew and Luke. Table 2.1 summarizes this arrangement. Column one

TABLE 2.1 Mark's Opening Narrative as it Appears in Matthew and Luke:
An Illustration of a Common Sequence of Stories in the Synoptic Gospels
The numbered events in Column One indicate the actual sequence of events in Mark.

Event	Mark	Matt	Luke
1. Proclamation of John the Baptist	1:1–8	3:1–12	3:1–20
2. Baptism of Jesus	1:9–11	3:13–17	3:21–22
Genealogy of Jesus in Luke		See 1:1–17	3:23–38
3. The temptation of Jesus	1:12–13	4::1–11	4:1–13
4. Beginning of Galilean Ministry	1:14–15	4:12–17	4:14–15
Rejection at Nazareth. Luke inserts this later Markan story out of order.	6:1–6	13:54–58	4:16–30
5. Jesus calls first disciples	1:16–20	4:18–22	5:1–11
6. Synagogue exorcism	1:21–28	Omitted	4:31–37
7. Simon's mother-in-law's fever	1:29–34	8:14–17	4:38–41
8. A preaching tour in Galilee	1:35–39	4:23–25	4:42–44
Sermon on the Mount		5–7	
9. Jesus cleanses a leper	1:40–45	8:1–4	5:12–16
10. Jesus heals paralytic	2:1–12	9:2–8	5:17–26
11. Jesus calls Matthew/Levi	2:13–17	9:9–13	5:27–32
12. Question about fasting	2:18–22	9:14–17	5:33–39

provides a short description of each event. Those incidents that have a number in front of them signify the actual sequence of stories in Mark. Those incidents without a number have no counterpart in the Markan sequence and indicate a disruption of Mark's narrative flow as it appears in either Matthew or Luke. The three other columns show the verse citations for where the stories appear in each of the three Gospels. By looking at the verse citations you can see which stories appear in the same order as each other and which stories diverge from the order in the other Gospels.

Matthew's Arrangement

Matthew records eleven of Mark's twelve stories in his Gospel and ten of those duplications appear in the same sequential order that Mark has. However, Matthew sometimes inserts other stories into the sequence so that all ten stories, while in the same narrative order, do not appear in the same connected manner as they do in Mark.

Taking a closer look, we see that Matthew repeats Mark's first five incidents in the same order without any disruption to the sequence followed by Mark. Matthew omits Mark's sixth incident, an exorcism in a synagogue, and places Mark's seventh story, the healing of Simon's mother-in-law's fever, into a later location in the narrative. After these two divergences from Mark's sequence, Matthew continues with Mark's eighth story, the preaching tour in Galilee.

At this point Matthew inserts the famous Sermon on the Mount, which appears in none of the other Gospels.[79] The Sermon is a lengthy undertaking, filling three chapters in Matthew, 5–7. At its conclusion Matthew returns again to Mark's sequence, relating Mark's ninth story about the cleansing of a leper. Between Mark's ninth and tenth stories Matthew inserts some additional material, including the displaced story of Simon's mother-in-law. Matthew follows this with Mark's last three incidents in the same narrative order, one after the other.

Matthew's three divergences from Mark's narrative—the elimination of Mark's sixth story about the exorcism in the synagogue, the relocation of the seventh story about Simon's mother-in-law, and the insertion of the Sermon on the Mount after the eighth story—all seem to have a thematic connection.

Let's look first at Mark's story of the exorcism of the demon in the synagogue. It can be divided into two parts, both of which take place on the same Sabbath day. According to Mark, Jesus first appears in the synagogue and delivers a sermon. At the conclusion of the sermon the attendees "were astounded at his teaching, for he taught them as one having authority, and not as the scribes" (Mark 1:22). In the second part, after receiving the congregation's recognition, a man possessed by a demon appears and Jesus orders the demon to leave the host. The crowd again remarks on Jesus' authority.

Mark's next story takes place immediately after the episode in the synagogue, on the same Sabbath day. Jesus and his initial disciples return to Simon's home where they find Simon's mother-in-law with a fever. Jesus takes her by the hand, lifts the woman up, and the fever dissipates.

Both of these Markan stories include healings on the Sabbath, a subject that becomes a major source of conflict later in all four Gospels. But in neither of Mark's stories does the issue get raised. Luke also places both stories on the Sabbath and he doesn't directly raise the Sabbath healing issues either. Matthew, on the other hand, has omitted the synagogue story from his Gospel and placed the story of Simon's mother-in-law on a non-Sabbath day.

While Matthew has no problem with describing exorcisms elsewhere in his Gospel, his omission of the Sabbath exorcism that appears in the other two Gospels suggests that he had problems with depicting Jesus conducting a Sabbath exorcism without any teaching by Jesus as to why such an action would be permissible. A similar concern seems to be present with the curing of the fever on the Sabbath. Matthew has eliminated the Sabbath healing issue by rearranging the narrative chronology so that the story takes place on a non-Sabbath day.

At the same time, while Matthew has omitted Mark's "sermon in the synagogue" story, at almost the identical place in Mark's narrative sequence Matthew has inserted the story of the Sermon on the Mount. At the end of Matthew's sermon story the crowd reacts to Jesus' teachings with the following words, "for he taught them as one having authority, and not as their scribes" (Matt 7:29). These are the same words used in Mark's story after the sermon in the synagogue. In Mark, the content of the sermon is omitted but Matthew has inserted a substantial collection of teachings to justify the praise heaped on Jesus.

What Matthew seems to have done is eliminate the exorcism portion of the synagogue story and move the highly-praised sermon from an indoor setting in the synagogue to an outdoor event on a non-Sabbath day, breaking the Sabbath connection. So for all practical purposes Matthew's Sermon on the Mount corresponds to Mark's synagogue story. In terms of sequential order Matthew places the sermon just after Jesus' preaching tour in Galilee while Mark sets it just before. Therefore, despite omitting the exorcism from the sermon story, Matthew's Gospel contains all twelve of Mark's opening twelve stories and has simply shifted the two Sabbath healing stories to slightly different locations to avoid the appearance that Jesus violated Jewish law. The remaining ten stories all appear in the same sequential order.

Luke's Arrangement

Luke hews more closely to Mark's narrative than Matthew does. He records all twelve of Mark's opening stories and has the same sequence as Mark for eleven of the twelve. Luke's only change to Mark's narrative order is the placement of the story about the recruiting of the first disciples, which Mark locates after his fifth story and Luke positions after Mark's eighth story, the preaching tour in Galilee. However, Luke does insert two other stories into Mark's narrative sequence.

One interruption to Mark's order of events takes place after telling us about the baptism of Jesus. Luke adds in a genealogy of Jesus that shows him to be descended from Adam (Luke 3:23–38.). Luke may have seen this as thematically related to the start of Jesus' mission and thought it necessary to inset this historical note at this point in the story. Mark has no such story in his own Gospel.

The second interruption occurs right after Jesus begins his ministry. He takes Mark's later story about Jesus being rejected at Nazareth (Mark 6:1–6) and locates it to just before the synagogue sermon where Jesus exorcises a demon. Mark's version of the rejection at Nazareth suggests that the incident was one of great embarrassment to Jesus and his disciples and implies that Jesus was rejected by his own family—"Prophets are not without honor, except in their hometown, and *among their own kin, and in their own house*" (Mark 6:4, emphasis added). Luke has significantly modified Mark's version of the story in many ways. Perhaps the most shocking is that he adds in an allegation (missing in Mark and Matthew) that the Nazareth Jews tried to kill Jesus by throwing him off a cliff. Some scholars have suggested that Luke moved this altered story of Jewish hostility to the beginning of Jesus' ministry in order to foreshadow Luke's later accusations of Jewish involvement in the death of Jesus.

In substance, then, all twelve of Mark's first dozen stories also appear in both Matthew and Luke. In Matthew, ten of twelve are in the same sequential order as Mark, and in Luke eleven of the twelve are in the same sequential order. Of the two stories in Matthew and one in Luke that are out of order, the rearrangement is trivial and suggests simple tinkering with a known order. But which of the three Gospels represent the original order and which of the three made minor changes to the order is part of the Synoptic Problem.

EVIDENCE OF VERBAL AGREEMENT IN THE TRIPLE TRADITION

Having seen how closely a large portion of all three Gospels follows the same narrative sequence lets now look at examples of significant verbal agreement among the three Synoptic Gospels. To illustrate, I will compare portions of Mark's ninth, tenth, and eleventh stories with the parallel accounts in Matthew and Luke. In all three Gospels these stories appear in the same sequential order. The three stories encompass the cleansing of a leper, the healing of a paralytic, and the calling of the Apostle Matthew (or Levi).

The Cleansing of the Leper

The story of Jesus cleansing a leper appears in Mark 1:40–45, Matt 8:1–4, and Luke 5:12–16. Table 2.2 shows all three versions of the story in a side-by-side manner. I have italicized certain portions of the text in order to focus on areas of verbal agreement.

In all three we find the following repetitive language:

- If you choose, you can make me clean.
- [. . .] stretched out his hand and touched him, [. . .]
- "I do choose. Be made clean!" Immediately [. . .]
- show yourself to the priest [. . .] Moses commanded [. . .] a testimony to them.

I have omitted some of the connecting language involving trivial variations. For example, after the word "immediately," Mark says "the leprosy left him, and he was made clean," while Matthew has "his leprosy was cleansed" and Luke says "Immediately the leprosy left him."

TABLE 2.2 Jesus Cures a Leper		
Mark 1:40–45	*Matt 8:1–4*	*Luke 5:12–16*
A leper came to him begging him, and kneeling he said to him, "*If you choose, you can make me clean.*" Moved with pity, Jesus *stretched out his hand and touched him, and said to him,* "*I do choose. Be made clean!*" *Immediately the leprosy left him,* and he was made clean. After sternly warning him he sent him away at once, saying to him, "*See that you say nothing to anyone; but go, show yourself to* the priest, and offer for your cleansing what *Moses commanded, as a testimony to them.*" But he went out and began to proclaim it freely, and to spread the word, so that Jesus could no longer go into a town openly, but stayed out in the country; and people came to him from every quarter.	When Jesus had come down from the mountain, great crowds followed him; and there was a leper who came to him and knelt before him, saying, "Lord, *if you choose, you can make me clean.*" He *stretched out his hand and touched him, saying,* "*I do choose. Be made clean!*" *Immediately his leprosy was cleansed.* Then Jesus said to him, "*See that you say nothing to anyone; but go, show yourself to the priest, and offer* the gift that *Moses commanded, as a testimony to them.*"	Once, when he was in one of the cities, there was a man covered with leprosy. When he saw Jesus, he bowed with his face to the ground and begged him, "Lord, *if you choose, you can make me clean.*" *Then Jesus stretched out his hand, touched him, and said,* "*I do choose. Be made clean.*" *Immediately the leprosy left him.* And he ordered him to tell no one. "*Go,*" he said, "*and show yourself to the priest, and,* as *Moses commanded,* make an *offering* for your cleansing, for *a testimony to them.*" But now more than ever the word about Jesus spread abroad; many crowds would gather to hear him and to be cured of their diseases. But he would withdraw to deserted places.

We also have examples where a phrase in Mark appears in Matthew but not in Luke or in Luke but not in Matthew. For example, Mark and Luke both say "Immediately the leprosy left him" while Matthew has "Immediately his leprosy was cleansed." Elsewhere, Mark and Matthew use the phrase "See that you say nothing to anyone" while Luke says "tell no one."

The Healing of the Paralytic

Our second set of parallel verses in Table 2.3 tells the story of Jesus healing a paralytic. The full versions of the story appear in Mark 2:1–

12, Matt 9:2–8, and Luke 5:17–28. I have left out some of the introductory material in Mark and Luke so that we can focus on the similar portions of the narrative. Again, I have italicized some of the text in order to focus on the verbal agreement. I have also placed a couple of

TABLE 2.3 Jesus Heals a Paralytic		
Mark 2:5–12	*Matt 9:2–8*	*Luke 5:20–26*
When Jesus saw their faith, he said to the paralytic, "Son, your sins are forgiven." Now some of the scribes were sitting there, questioning in their hearts, "Why does this fellow speak in this way? It is blasphemy! *Who can forgive sins but God alone?"* At once *Jesus perceived* in his spirit that they were discussing these questions among themselves; and he said to them, *"Why do you raise such questions in your hearts? Which is easier, to say to the paralytic, 'Your sins are forgiven,' or to say,* **'Stand up and take your mat and walk'?** *But so that you may know that the Son of Man has authority on earth to forgive sins"*—he said to the paralytic— *"I say to you,* **stand up, take your mat** *and go to your home." And he stood up, and immediately took the mat and went out before all of them; so that they were all amazed and glorified God,* saying, "We have never seen anything like this!"	*When Jesus saw their faith, he said to the paralytic,* "Take heart, *son; your sins are forgiven."* Then some of the scribes said to themselves, "This man is blaspheming." But *Jesus, perceiving* their thoughts, said, *"Why do you think evil in your hearts? For which is easier, to say, 'Your sins are forgiven,' or to say,* **'Stand up and walk?'** *But so that you may know that the Son of Man has authority on earth to forgive sins"*—he then said to the paralytic— **"Stand up, take your bed** *and go to your home." And he stood up and went to his home.* When the crowds saw it, *they were filled with awe, and they glorified God,* who had given such authority to human beings.	*When he saw their faith, he said,* "Friend *your sins are forgiven you."* Then the scribes and the Pharisees began to question, "Who is this who is speaking blasphemies? *Who can forgive sins but God alone?"* When *Jesus perceived* their questionings, he answered them, *"Why do you raise such questions in your hearts? Which is easier, to say, 'Your sins are forgiven you,' or to say,* **'Stand up and walk?'** *But so that you may know that the Son of Man has authority on earth to forgive sins"*—he said to the one who was paralyzed— *"I say to you,* **stand up and take your bed** *and go to your home." Immediately he stood up before them, took* what he had been lying on, *and went to his home, glorifying God. Amazement seized all of them, and they glorified God and were filled with awe,* saying, "We have seen strange things today."

words in bold face to point out two related minor instances where Matthew and Luke agree against Mark.

Here again we see the repetition of phrases in all three versions.

- When [. . .] saw their faith, he said [. . .]"your sins are forgiven."
- Which is easier, to say [. . .] 'Your sins are forgiven,' or to say, 'Stand up . . . and walk?
- But so that you may know that the Son of Man has authority on earth to forgive sins.
- Stand up and take your [mat/bed] and go to your home.
- He stood up . . . and went.

We also see evidence of word agreement in two Gospels against the third. Mark and Luke both have the scribes say "Who can forgive sins but God alone?" but this phrase is missing in Matthew. Mark and Matthew both have the phrase "he said to the paralytic" but Luke omits "to the paralytic."

On the other hand, we have some minor instances in which Matthew and Luke agree against Mark. At Mark 2:9, the author uses the phrase "stand up and take your mat and walk." In the corresponding passages at Matt 9:5 and Luke 5:23, both Gospels omit "and take your mat." In a similar variation at Mark 2:11, Jesus says to the paralytic, "I say to you, stand up, take your mat and go to your home." At the corresponding points in Matt 9:6 and Luke 5:24, both authors substitute "bed" for "mat." However, Luke and Matthew use slightly different versions of the same Greek word for "bed," suggesting that the one did not copy from the other but that each independently thought that the Greek word for "bed" was a slightly better word than the different word Mark used.[80]

The Recruiting of the Apostle Matthew/Levi

Our final set of verses in Table 2.4 tells of Jesus recruiting the Apostle Matthew. The stories appear in Mark 2:14–17, Matt 9:9–13, and Luke 5:27–32. An interesting distinction in the stories is the variation in the Apostle's name. Only Matthew refers to the Apostle as Matthew. Mark calls him "Levi, son of Alphaeus" and Luke simply calls him "Levi." This

TABLE 2.4 The Calling of Levi/Matthew		
Mark 2:14–17	Matt 9:9–13	Luke 5:27–32
As he was walking along, he saw Levi son of Alphaeus sitting at the tax booth, and he said to him, "Follow me." And he got up and followed him. And as he sat at dinner in Levi's house, many tax collectors and sinners were also sitting with Jesus and his disciples —for there were many who followed him. When the scribes of the Pharisees saw that he was eating with sinners and tax collectors, they said to his disciples, "Why does he eat_ with tax collectors and sinners?" Then Jesus heard this, he said to them, "Those who are well have no need of a physician, but those who are sick; I have come to call not the righteous but sinners."	After this he went out and saw a tax collector named Levi, sitting at the tax booth; and he said to him, "Follow me." And he got up, left everything, and followed him. Then Levi gave a great banquet for him in his house; and there was a large crowd of tax collectors and others sitting at the table with them. The Pharisees and their scribes were complaining to his disciples, saying, "Why do you eat and drink with tax collectors and sinners?" Jesus answered, "Those who are well have no need of a physician, but those who are sick; I have come to call not the righteous but sinners to repentance."	As Jesus was walking along, he saw a man called Matthew sitting at the tax booth; and he said to him, "Follow me." And he got up and followed him. And as he sat at dinner in the house, many tax collectors and sinners came and were sitting with him and his disciples. When the Pharisees saw this, they said to his disciples, "Why does your teacher eat with tax collectors and sinners?" But when he heard this, he said, "Those who are well have no need of a physician, but those who are sick. Go and learn what this means, 'I desire mercy, not sacrifice.' For I have come to call not the righteous but sinners."

time I did not italicize corresponding words because of the high degree of agreement throughout the story.

Markan Priority

The large amount of agreement among the three Gospels as to story, word usage and sequence very strongly suggests that there must have been some written source for the Triple Tradition.[81] This would indicate that either all three Gospels had access to a similar written source that preceded the

Gospels or that one of the written Gospels had some sort of source relationship to the other two. In the latter case that would mean either two of the Gospel authors, independently of each other, used the third Gospel as a source, or one of the Gospel authors used one of the other Gospels as a source and the third author used at least one of the other two as a source. In attempting to unravel the relationships we have a number of clues.

While we have seen that there is a significant amount of sequential agreement in the order of the stories we occasionally find differences in the sequences in one Gospel or the other. In such instances we almost always find that either both Mark and Matthew agree against Luke or that both Mark and Luke agree against Matthew. But rarely do both Matthew and Luke agree against Mark.

In our analysis of the first twelve stories in Mark, for example, we saw that Luke differs from Mark with regard to when Jesus called the first disciples but Matthew agrees with Mark on the sequential order. At the same time Matthew disagrees with Mark about when the incident with Simon's mother-in-law took place while Luke agrees with Mark. In no instance do Matthew and Luke share the same sequence of events in disagreement with Mark's order of the first twelve stories. Many other examples exist throughout the Gospels.

A similar set of correlations exist on verbal agreements. On those occasions where there is a difference among the Gospels as to the language used within a common story we usually find either both Mark and Matthew agree against Luke or both Mark and Luke agree against Matthew. But rarely do Matthew and Luke disagree against Mark.

These are two of the major reasons why scholars almost universally believe that Mark was written before either Matthew or Luke. Another argument in favor of Markan priority is that Mark has a less elegant form of Greek than Matthew or Luke, and if he were copying from the others it is unlikely that he would render their Greek in a more primitive fashion. Scholars also wonder why Mark would omit so much material from Matthew and Luke in his own account if he had used either one of them for a source.

As a starting point then, scholars accept that Mark was written first and that at least one of the other Gospel authors relied on Mark as a source.[82] It is possible, however, that Mark also relied on a written source similar to his own and that it was this Markan source that Matthew and Luke used rather than Mark himself. This could explain why a significant portion of Mark was omitted from Matthew and Luke. If Mark occasionally made some changes to this earlier source text it could also explain why Matthew and Luke might occasionally agree against Mark on some occasions. While the idea of an undiscovered proto-Mark can't be easily dismissed, the existence of our written Mark makes it difficult to reject the idea that Mark's Gospel was the written source underlying Matthew and Luke.

ANOTHER ARGUMENT FOR MARKAN PRIORITY

In this section I want to look at an example of the literary interplay between the Synoptic Gospels and how it offers a further clue as to Markan priority and the use of Mark by both Matthew and Luke. I will use the story of Jesus curing the fever of Simon's mother-in-law for our analysis. The account appears in Mark 1:29–31, Matt 8:14–15 and Luke 4:38–39. It is very brief, no more than three verses in any of the Gospels. But despite the brevity the three versions exhibit significant differences that offer important clues as to the literary relationship among the three Gospels.

In Mark's version, Jesus and some of his disciples leave the synagogue (where the exorcism had just occurred) on the Sabbath and go to the house of Simon (i.e., the Apostle Peter). Inside the house Simon's mother-in-law is feverish. Jesus takes her by the hand and lifts her up. The fever leaves, the mother-in-law gets up and serves the guests a meal. Mark omits any discussion of whether lifting the mother-in-law or healing her on the Sabbath constituted a violation of the Sabbath laws and none of the Jews in attendance asks any questions about it. Later, in Mark 3:1–6, healing on the Sabbath triggers a major religious clash between Jesus and the Pharisees.

Matthew, as we saw above, had this story in a different chronological sequence from Mark and placed it on a non-Sabbath day. Together with other evidence we saw that Matthew seemed to have a problem with having Jesus healing someone on the Sabbath. Matthew also eliminated the lifting of the woman from Mark's story and simply had Jesus touch the mother-in-law. After the cure she gets up and, as in Mark, serves a meal.

Luke, like Mark, places the story on the Sabbath but unlike Mark there is no lifting and unlike Matthew there is no touching. Jesus simply stands over the woman. In Luke the fever is caused by a demon and Jesus rebukes the demon. The demon departs, the woman is cured, and she gets up and fixes a meal.

If Matthew were the first Gospel and either Mark or Luke used Matthew as a source, why would either of them change Matthew's non-Sabbath story so that it takes place on a Sabbath and raise the issue of possible Sabbath violations, especially when we are talking about a story that consists of just two verses. It seems highly unlikely that this would occur. It just doesn't seem to make much sense.

This strongly suggests that either Mark or Luke preceded Matthew, and that Matthew thought that the Sabbath setting created legal issues. It is easy to understand how Matthew could think that. We know that in all four Gospels healing on the Sabbath eventually becomes a major point of contention between Jesus and the Pharisees. In all such conflicts, however, Jesus always explained why he wouldn't be violating the Sabbath law. In this fever story Jesus makes no such argument. He doesn't even address the issue.

Absent a teaching by Jesus as to why the potential violation would be lawful, it seems much more likely that Matthew would remove a potential Sabbath violation than that Mark or Luke would deliberately add in a potential Sabbath violation. In support of this notion we should recall that Matthew is also missing the story of the Sabbath exorcism in the synagogue that appears in both Mark and Luke. This suggests that either Mark and/or Luke preceded Matthew and that either Mark used Luke or Luke used Mark as a source.

Further analysis shows that Mark likely preceded Luke. In Matthew, Jesus touches the woman but doesn't lift her, and the fever is cured. In Luke, Jesus neither touches nor lifts the woman but exorcises a demon and the woman is cured. In Mark, we have touching, lifting and a cure, but no exorcism.

If Mark post-dated Matthew (which implies from the above analysis that Luke must have preceded Matthew) Mark could have gotten the touching from Matthew. But if that were the case, where did Mark get the lifting of the woman from? It doesn't appear in Matthew or Luke. This is an important issue because lifting someone on the Sabbath is potentially a serious Sabbath violation. At the very least we should expect Jesus to explain why this was a lawful act. But Mark has no such teaching. This suggests that either Mark added the lifting to Luke's story or Luke removed the lifting from Mark's story. We'll come back to this in a moment but let's first examine the exorcism issue.

In Luke the fever is cured by an exorcism. Mark has no exorcism. Both Gospels, however, place this story immediately after the Sabbath synagogue exorcism. In that story we also have no explanation by Jesus as to why his actions are lawful. Nevertheless, both Gospel authors appear comfortable with Jesus performing an exorcism on the Sabbath in order to cure an illness. In fact, in a story appearing only in Luke 13:10–17, Jesus conducts a Sabbath exorcism and gives a legal argument for why in that case it was permissible.

As with the lifting of the woman, then, we are left with these options. Either Mark copied from Luke and removed Luke's exorcism on the Sabbath, even though Mark clearly had no problem with a Sabbath exorcism, and substituted a very problematic Sabbath lifting and touching, or Luke copied from Mark and replaced a very problematic lifting and healing by touch with a non-problematic (to Luke and Mark) Sabbath exorcism.

It seems highly unlikely that in a story of only two verses that Mark would seek to create so many problems by eliminating what he considered to be a proper action by Jesus. If he copied from Luke it makes no sense for him to replace the exorcism (which he accepted in the immediately preceding incident in the synagogue) and substitute touching and lifting (neither of which appears in Luke's version) without any kind of explanation by Jesus or even any inquiry from the Jews in attendance. The most likely occurrence from a literary/historical analysis is that Luke must have amended Mark rather than the other way around.

In summary, then, our analysis shows that either Mark and/or Luke must have preceded Matthew and that Mark likely preceded Luke. This indicates that Mark must have been the first Gospel and that both Matthew and Luke must have copied from Mark. This still leaves open the relationship between Luke and Matthew.

Q AND THE "DOUBLE TRADITION" IN MATTHEW AND LUKE

While scholars almost universally accept Markan priority, we still have a secondary problem. How do we account for the Double Tradition, those portions of Matthew and Luke that seem to agree with each other but do not appear in Mark?

Table 2.5 compares five such examples in Matthew and Luke. The verses are arranged in the order that they appear in Luke. The degree of verbal coincidence in these examples is extremely high but not all the textual units in the Double Tradition show this same level of agreement. Notice also that four of the five Matthew verses appear in the same sequential order as in Luke. If we re-arranged the order to follow Matthew's sequence, four of the five Luke passages would appear in the same order as Matthew. As we have seen from our discussion of the Triple Tradition, while the authors of Matthew and Luke may have shared a common written source in Mark, neither was above occasionally changing the order of stories from that in their source.

An interesting subset of the Double Tradition problem concerns certain verbal themes in the Triple Tradition that reappear in a second location in just Matthew and Luke. For example, Mark 8:34 quote Jesus as saying "If any want to become my followers, let them deny themselves and take up their cross and follow me." The same quote appears in Matt 16:24 and Luke 9:23. Elsewhere, however, Matt 10:38 quotes Jesus as saying "whoever does not take up the cross

TABLE 2.5 Examples of Verbal Agreement Between Matthew and Luke in the Double Tradition

Matthew	Luke
John the Baptist addresses the crowd	
But when he saw many Pharisees and Sadducees coming for baptism, he said to them, "You brood of vipers! Who warned you to flee from the wrath to come? Bear fruit worthy of repentance. Do not presume to say to yourselves, 'We have Abraham as our ancestor'; for I tell you, God is able from these stones to raise up children to Abraham. Even now the ax is lying at the root of the trees; every tree therefore that does not bear good fruit is cut down and thrown into the fire. —Matt 3:7–10	John said to the crowds that came out to be baptized by him, "You brood of vipers! Who warned you to flee from the wrath to come? Bear fruits worthy of repentance. Do not begin to say to yourselves, 'We have Abraham as our ancestor'; for I tell you, God is able from these stones to raise up children to Abraham. Even now the ax is lying at the root of the trees; every tree therefore that does not bear good fruit is cut down and thrown into the fire." —Luke 3:7–9
Jesus talks about John	
As they went away, Jesus began to speak to the crowds about John: "What did you go out into the wilderness to look at? A reed shaken by the wind? What then did you go out to see? Someone dressed in soft robes? Look, those who wear soft robes are in royal palaces. What then did you go out to see? A prophet? Yes, I tell you, and more than a prophet. This is the one about whom it is written, 'See, I am sending my messenger ahead of you, who will prepare your way before you.' —Matt: 11:7–10	When John's messengers had gone, Jesus began to speak to the crowds about John: "What did you go out into the wilderness to look at? A reed shaken by the wind? What then did you go out to see? Someone dressed in soft robes? Look, those who put on fine clothing and live in luxury are in royal palaces. What then did you go out to see? A prophet? Yes, I tell you, and more than a prophet. This is the one about whom it is written, 'See, I am sending my messenger ahead of you, who will prepare your way before you.' —Luke 7:24–27.

and follow me is not worthy of me," and Luke 14:27 has the phrase, "Whoever does not carry the cross and follow me cannot be my disciple." Mark has no similar quote. There is a slight verbal shift in perspective in the second set of quotes. The Markan version tells a poten-

Matthew	Luke
Would-be followers of Jesus	
Now when Jesus saw great crowds around him, he gave orders to go over to the other side. A scribe then approached and said, "Teacher, I will follow you wherever you go." And Jesus said to him, "Foxes have holes, and birds of the air have nests; but the Son of Man has nowhere to lay his head." Another of his disciples said to him, "Lord, first let me go and bury my father." But Jesus said to him, "Follow me, and let the dead bury their own dead." —*Matt 8:18–22*	As they were going along the road, someone said to him, "I will follow you wherever you go." And Jesus said to him, "Foxes have holes, and birds of the air have nests; but the Son of Man has nowhere to lay his head." To another he said, "Follow me." But he said, "Lord, first let me go and bury my father." But Jesus said to him, "Let the dead bury their own dead; but as for you, go and proclaim the kingdom of God." —*Luke 9:57–60*
Jesus Rejoices	
At that time Jesus said, "I thank you, Father, Lord of heaven and earth, because you have hidden these things from the wise and the intelligent and have revealed them to infants; yes, Father, for such was your gracious will. All things have been handed over to me by my Father; and no one knows the Son except the Father, and no one knows the Father except the Son and anyone to whom the Son chooses to reveal him. —*Matt 11:25–27*	At that same hour Jesus rejoiced in the Holy Spirit and said, "I thank you, Father, Lord of heaven and earth, because you have hidden these things from the wise and the intelligent and have revealed them to infants; yes, Father, for such was your gracious will. All things have been handed over to me by my Father; and no one knows who the Son is except the Father, or who the Father is except the Son and anyone to whom the Son chooses to reveal him. —*Luke 10:21–22*
The Lament over Jerusalem	
Jerusalem, Jerusalem, the city that kills the prophets and stones those who are sent to it! How often have I desired to gather your children together as a hen gathers her brood under her wings, and you were not willing! See, your house is left to you, desolate, For I tell you, you will not see me again until you say, 'Blessed is the one who comes in the name of the Lord.'" —*Matt 23:37–39*	Jerusalem, Jerusalem, the city that kills the prophets and stones those who are sent to it! How often have I desired to gather your children together as a hen gathers her brood under her wings, and you were not willing! See, your house is left to you. And I tell you, you will not see me until the time comes when you say, 'Blessed is the one who comes in the name of the Lord.'" —*Luke 13:34–35*

tial follower what he should do while the non-Markan version tells a potential follower what he shouldn't do.

In another example, Mark 4:25 reads "For to those who have, more will be given; and from those who have nothing, even what they have will be taken away." The identical quote appears in Matt 13:12 and Luke 8:18. Later, Matt 25:29 and Luke 19:26, each recounting the Parable of the Talents, which doesn't appear in Mark, both use the same phrase again, although Matthew has inserted a couple of extra words into it.[83] That the second set of verses should appear in the same context in Matthew and Luke, which setting is absent in Mark, should suggests that there may have been multiple sources for this quote, one in Mark and one from somewhere else, either Matthew, Luke or a third source.

The existence of this Double Tradition set of textual units strongly suggests that there is some sort of literary relationship between Matthew and Luke. The dominant view is that Matthew and Luke shared a common written source and wrote independently of each other; neither knew the other's Gospel.[84] The many long stretches of verbal agreement suggest that there must have been a written document.[85] New Testament scholars refer to this written source as Q. Unfortunately, no Q document has ever been discovered and its existence, highly theoretical, is pieced together from the Double Tradition. Some scholars have suggested that Matthew and Luke may have had different versions of Q that didn't fully agree with each other.[86]

Q scholarship constitutes a major branch of New Testament studies and is the subject of much debate and many questions. Among the chief issues raised are such matters as the original written language of Q, Aramaic or Greek; the original order of the verses; and whether it was a single composition or went through various redactional stages. There are also obvious questions about what particular textual units belong to the theoretical Q and when it (or its various stages) was written. It is possible for example, that on some occasions only Matt or only Luke may have quoted from Q, in which case we wouldn't have the Double Tradition clue indicating a common source. If one omitted portions of Q present in the other, Q may be longer and more extensive than presently accepted. Within this context, Bart Ehrman, a leading expert on ancient Christian manuscripts, cautions, "Notwithstanding the extravagant claims of some scholars, we simply do not know the full extent or character of Q. . . . It is probably best for methodological purposes to simply define it strictly as material shared by Matthew and Luke that is not also found in Mark."[87]

As to the original language, Kloppenborg, after reviewing the various arguments, contends that the evidence strongly favors a Greek original.[88] He also proposes, as do most Q scholars, that the order of the sayings in Luke is more likely to represent the original sequence of sayings than does Matthew.[89] Many scholars believe that Q consisted of two major levels of development and that subsequently someone added in a third passage that differs somewhat in form from the earlier portions.[90] This third element consists entirely of the story of Jesus' temptation in the wilderness (a much longer version than appears in Mark—compare Mark 1:12–13 with Matt 4:1–11 and Luke 4:1–13) and is more of a narrative than the rest of Q.[91] As to the date of composition, most scholars would probably place it close in time to Mark but any more precise date is hard to come by.[92]

Thematically, Q represents a "sayings" or "wisdom" source, consisting mostly of teachings by Jesus. One of the interesting aspects of Q, at least as it is recovered from the Double Tradition in Matthew and Luke, is that it contains no accounts of either the baptism of Jesus or the crucifixion or Resurrection.[93] This raises some questions as to how influential these three events were in the earliest stages of the Jesus movement.

For a good overview of the Q thesis I would recommend *The Formation of Q* by John S. Kloppenborg. For the argument against Q a useful work would be *The Case against Q* by Mark Goodacre.

SUMMARY

The question of why there is so much sequential and verbal agreement in the Gospels of Matthew, Mark and Luke is known as the Synoptic Problem. The dominant solution holds that Mark was the first of the written

Gospels and that Matthew and Luke, writing independently of each other, used Mark as a source and also used a lost document scholars refer to as Q. In this chapter we looked at some of the evidence that gives rise to the Synoptic Problem and looked at several examples of sequential and verbal agreement within the three Gospels that strongly suggested that at least two of the Gospels used at least one of the other Gospels as a source.

We began with a look at the first twelve stories in the Gospel of Mark and saw that all twelve stories appeared in the Gospel of Luke, with eleven stories in the same sequential order as Mark and with very little disruption to Mark's narrative flow. We also saw that Matthew obviously had eleven of the twelve stories and also appeared to have the twelfth story in a significantly altered form. Here, too, we found little disruption to Mark's narrative flow.

We also took a close look at three consecutive stories from this narrative and compared the verbal content. We found several examples of verbal agreement within the stories and some evidence suggesting that Mark was written prior to Matthew and Luke. We also analyzed the elements of the story of Simon's mother-in-law and saw logical evidence that suggested Markan priority with regard to that story.

We then turned our attention to the matter of sequential and verbal agreement within those passages appearing within Matthew and Luke but not in Mark. Again we saw evidence for both phenomena, suggesting some sort of literary relationship between the two Gospels. The primary proposal with regard to those passages is that there existed an early written "sayings of Jesus" source that included some additional material and that both Luke and Matthew, independently of each other, made use of that written source in writing their respective Gospels.

CHAPTER 3

Did the Author
of John Know
the Synoptic Gospels?

The author of the Gospel of John seems to be familiar with many of the stories in the Synoptic Gospels. In some cases he knows a story with similar factual details or some factual variations not unlike some of the differences between Mark and Matthew or Luke but sometimes he seems to know a story that seems to have only some sort of symbolical or metaphoric relationship to a Synoptic story but factually looks to be very different. Sometimes, when he tells a story that varies factually from the Synoptic Gospels he knows a detail from one of the three stories that doesn't appear in the other two. Sometimes it's an item from Mark, sometimes Matthew, sometimes Luke. On occasion, a story that appears in one of the Synoptic Gospels seems to be divided into separate pieces and redistributed throughout John. The Gospel of John also seems to share with Luke several interesting story elements that don't appear in Mark or Matthew, especially with regard to the Passion.

These parallel instances between John and one or the other of the Synoptic Gospels raise the issue of whether John knew one or more of the Synoptic Gospels and, if so, which ones. On the other hand, many of the stories that appear in John and one or the other of the Synoptic Gospels may have been well-known in Christian circles and variations may have set in as the stories circulated around in oral or written form. Also, John's literary style is very unlike the Synoptic Gospels. He has long christological discourses about Jesus' identity, he makes no mention of the exorcisms that are frequent in the Synoptic Gospels, and he doesn't seem to refer to the many parables found in the other Gospels. John also reflects a very different chronological perspective as to the unfolding of events, showing, at least on the surface level, a three-year mission with multiple journeys to Jerusalem where the Synoptic Gospels depict a short-mission, less than a year, taking place almost exclusively outside of Jerusalem except for the final week of Jesus' life.

The literary relationship of John to the Synoptic Gospels is far more contentious in New Testament studies than is the widely-accepted solution to the Synoptic Problem. According to Raymond Brown, a leading expert on Johannine studies, the dominant view in the middle of the twentieth century was that John had no connection to the Synoptic Gospels but that towards the latter part of the century growing support for some form of Synoptic dependence has reduced that dominant position to a small majority.[94] For all practical purposes, we can probably say that there is a split down the middle on whether or not John used or at least knew any of the Synoptic Gospels.

The question of Synoptic dependence is not the only major conflict among scholars with regard to the development of the Gospel of John. One big issue is whether the Gospel was primarily the work of a single individual or more than one individual.[95] A related question is whether the Gospel was written primarily as a single document with some possible minor tweaking or was developed in stages. Brown says one fairly popular view holds that there may have been at least two different major authors of the Gospel of John, one commonly called the Evangelist and the other the Redactor.[96] The Redactor is often thought also to be the author of the Johannine Epistles in the New Testament.[97]

Another subject of great debate is the nature of John's sources. A fairly common approach among Johannine scholars is to posit at least three major sources that influenced the development of John.[98]

One is a "Signs" source, a collection of miracles performed by Jesus. That was probably intended to induce doubters to follow Jesus.[99] A clue in this regard is that John 2:11 and 4:54 use the expressions "the first of his signs" and "this was the second sign" along with John 20:30, which says that "Jesus did many other signs in the presence of his disciples." This suggested that John drew upon the list of signs in this theoretical source and omitted some of them from his Gospel. On the other hand, several of the subsequent miracles after the second sign, are not designated as numbered miracles, and the author of John may have just numbered the first two signs for emphasis.

Another theoretical category is a "Revelatory Discourse" source.[100] In John there are several long poetic style discourses filled with metaphors and theological propositions. It is thought that there might have been a collection of such discourses and John adapted them to his own purposes. Included in this collection may have been the prologue to John, the only Gospel section that talks about the pre-existence of Jesus at the Creation.

Finally, there may have been an independent "Passion and Resurrection" source.[101] John's account of these events varies in many ways from the Synoptics and contains material not present in the Synoptics. It is primarily with the Passion account in John that we see many possible parallels in Luke that are missing in Mark and Matthew.[102] For example, in Luke and John, Pilate declares Jesus innocent on three different occasions; Mark and Matthew have no such declarations by Pilate, although Matthew 27:19 suggests a later trend moving in that direction. If there was this alternative Passion source underlying part of John's Passion account, did Luke also know it or were the similarities due to either coincidence or the copying by one Gospel author from the other?

Other areas of great difficulty for Johannine scholars encompass the many sequential breaks and inconsistencies with odd chronological jumps.[103] For example, in the Synoptics Jesus makes only one Passover visit to Jerusalem, in John there are three such visits and some of the events described in the single visit in Mark are distributed throughout the three separate visits in John. The Johannine version suggests a three-year mission as opposed to less than one year in Mark. Did John take a story about a single visit in Jerusalem and break it down to three separate visits? Did Mark take a series of three separate visits and combine them into one?

If John did divide a single Jerusalem trip into three separate visits did he want the reader to understand these as three separate visits or was he just rearranging the material for thematic purposes to make a theological point, knowing full well that the three separate accounts are all about a single visit. Think of it like a movie that moves the plot forward with flashbacks or time shifts. The director doesn't necessarily want you to think of the unfolding scenes as a straight chronological narrative; he presents events out of order so that you can see things from a different perspective that leads to a unified conclusion.

With most issues relating to the development of the Gospel of John you will probably get a lot of debate from opposing groups of respected scholars. In this chapter we will look at some examples of the sort of issues that arise from a study of John in relationship to the Synoptic Gospels.

THE ANOINTING AT BETHANY

A good example of Gospel texts that raise questions about the relationship between John and the Synoptics can be found in the story of the Anointing at Bethany. Versions of this story appear in all four Gospels (Mark 14:3–9; Matt 26:6–13; Luke 7:36–50; John 12:1–8). They provide an interesting illustration of how John seems to touch on all three Synoptic Gospels while also showing us how the Evangelists may have edited their sources for theological or political reasons.

In three of the Gospels the story is closely associated with the events leading up to the Passion. The scene in question describes the anointing of Jesus with expensive ointment, criticism of the anointing, and a problematic remark by Jesus about the plight of the poor. Mark and Matthew place the event immediately before the story in which Judas goes to the priests to betray Jesus. John has a similar story that occurs a few days before the betrayal. Luke has relocated the story to a much earlier time in Jesus' mission and has radically transformed the account so that it is almost unrecognizable as the same event in the other Gospels.

Mark's Version (Mark 14:3–9)

The earliest version of the story appears in Mark. It takes place after Jesus' arrival in Jerusalem for the Passover holiday, but the narrative chronology is a little vague. The event occurs either one or two days before Passover

(Mark 14:1, 14:12). Mark tells us that Jesus stayed at the house of Simon the leper in Bethany. While seated at the table, an unidentified woman carrying an alabaster jar containing "costly ointment of nard" approached Jesus, broke open the jar and poured the ointment over his head. Some of the people present weren't happy with the woman's actions. According to Mark,

> But some were there who said to one another in anger, "Why was the ointment wasted in this way? For this ointment could have been sold for more than three hundred denarii, and the money given to the poor." And they scolded her. (Mark 14:4–5)

Jesus did not agree with this assessment and responded with a strange rebuke.

> Let her alone; why do you trouble her? She has performed a good service for me. *For you always have the poor with you, and you can show kindness to them whenever you wish; but you will not always have me.* She has done what she could; she has anointed my body beforehand for its burial. Truly I tell you, wherever the good news is proclaimed in the whole world, what she has done will be told in remembrance of her. (Mark 14:6–9, emphasis added)

There are several salient features in this story to keep in mind as we review the other versions of this incident in the other Gospels.

- The woman who pours the ointment is unidentified.
- The woman pours the oil on Jesus' head.
- The oil is very expensive and a specific value of 300 denarii is recorded, presumably to emphasize to the reader how valuable the oil was.[104]
- Unidentified people present complain about this action and argue that the oil could have been sold and the money used to help the poor.
- The woman is scolded by the complainers.
- Jesus rebukes the complainers, dismissing their concern for the poor in what might be considered a callous manner.

- Jesus makes it clear that he understands that he is about to die within a very short period of time.

The pouring of oil over Jesus' head would normally be understood as the anointing of a king, consistent with the general theme that Jesus is the Messiah. ("Christ" is the Greek term for the Hebrew word "Messiah," which means "the anointed one.") However, in Mark's Gospel there is never any public claim by Jesus that he is the Messiah.[105] It is a major theme in Mark's Gospel that no human truly understands who Jesus is while he is alive—not even Peter, who misunderstands the heavenly role of Jesus (Mark 8:33)—and that the true nature of Jesus is only revealed by the events surrounding his death.

Such an anointing would also raise political problems as it would suggest that Pilate was correct in executing Jesus for claiming to be king. Therefore, Mark, true to his theme, needs to undercut the messianic nature of the anointing. So he has Jesus remark that the anointing is for the purpose of his burial. This would imply that he is just a few hours away from burial but he doesn't die for another one to three days (Mark 14:1). So the anointing for the purpose of a burial makes little sense in Mark's narrative.

Matthew's Version (Matt 26:6–13)

Matthew closely follows the contours of Mark's anointing story but incorporates some subtle changes. First, Matthew omits the price of the oil. He simply says that it was "very costly" and could be "sold for a large sum." He also omits Mark's description of the oil as "nard." One gets the impression that the cost of the oil embarrassed Matthew and that he felt a need to downplay its true value.

The most significant change, however, is that instead of "some" complaining in anger, Matthew says it was the "disciples" who reacted in such a manner, but he doesn't say which ones made the complaint. Why did Matthew change Mark's anonymous "some" to the more specific "disciples"? We'll return to that question shortly.

Luke's Version (Luke 7:36–50)

Luke transfers the story to a much earlier point in Jesus' mission and radically alters the content. In Luke's account the location is unclear but the incident does also takes place in the house of someone named Simon, but here Simon is identified as a Pharisee (Luke 7:39–40). In Mark, the story takes place in the house of Simon the Leper (Mark 14:3). Whether Luke's Simon was also a leper, as in Mark's version, we don't know.

In this version, the woman is still unidentified but she is now described as a sinner. As in Mark's account she also carried an alabaster jar of ointment and approached Jesus. But after approaching Jesus Luke departs from Mark. In Luke, the woman bathes Jesus' feet with her tears and dries them with her hair. She then kissed his feet and applied the ointment to the feet instead of the head. Luke also omits any reference to the value of the ointment and no one complains that the money spent on the ointment could be better used for the poor. Instead, the Pharisees at the dinner table complain that if Jesus were truly a prophet he wouldn't be associating with this sinner.

Jesus rebukes the Pharisees, claiming that this woman had shown him more love and devotion than his host and that her sins were forgiven. Some of the guests discussed amongst themselves who Jesus was that he could forgive sins. Jesus' rebuke has omitted the reference to the poor always being with us and, not surprisingly given the much earlier chronological setting, there is no reference to his imminent burial.

Luke's radical reconstruction of the story omits the problematic issue of Jesus appearing callous towards the poor and more concerned with his own personal comfort. The woman has been transformed into a sinner, presumably one of the poor that Jesus dismisses in Mark's version. Luke also omits the price of the oil. These changes suggest that, like Matthew, the author may have been disturbed by the apparent extravagance of Jesus and his seeming lack of concern for the poor. Luke's repositioning also breaks Mark's connection between this incident and Judas' meeting with the priests.

Perhaps the most important change, however, is that the woman anoints Jesus on the feet instead of over the head. This eliminated the problem of the audience associating the anointing with the inauguration of a messiah/king.

Despite Luke's radical changes to Mark's plot, certain story elements show that Luke is depending, at least in part, on Mark as a source for this account. He preserves Mark's references to a woman with an alabaster jar of ointment, a house belonging to a man named Simon, the application of the ointment to Jesus' body, anger by those present at some aspect of the anointing, Jesus chastising the complainers, and Jesus praising the woman.

John's Version (John 12:1–8)

Let's now look at John's very interesting take on this story. John seems to know the same basic story as Mark and closely parallels it, but, like Luke, he has some significant variations from Mark's account.

John, like Mark, locates the story in Bethany but not in the house of Simon the Leper. He places it in the home of Lazarus, whom, John alleges, Jesus had earlier raised from the dead. He places the event six days before the Passover holiday and before the triumphal entry into Jerusalem, a slight variation from Mark's chronology, which depicts the anointing as taking place after the triumphal entry and perhaps a day or two before the arrest of Jesus. John's chronology, as in Luke, breaks Mark's direct link between the anointing scene and the specific act of Judas consulting with the priests immediately thereafter.

John identifies the woman as Mary, the sister of Lazarus, and she "took a pound of costly perfume made of pure nard, anointed Jesus' feet, and wiped them with her hair. The house was filled with the fragrance of the perfume" (John 12:3). Both John and Luke indicate the woman anointed Jesus over the feet and dried his feet with her hair. (In Luke she dries tears off the feet and then anoints; in John she anoints and then dries.)

At this point John introduces Judas into the scene.

> But Judas Iscariot, one of his disciples (the one who was about to betray him), said, "Why was this perfume not sold for three hundred denarii and the money given to the poor?" (John 12:4–5)

John agrees with Mark that the oil was made from nard and cost 300 denarii. But he diverges from Mark as to the identity of the complainer. Mark had an unidentified "some"; Matthew changed it to the more specific identification of the "disciples" as a group; John narrows the identification down to a single disciple, Judas.

Immediately after this disclosure, John adds a significant gloss to the story. He says of Judas, "He said this not because he cared about the poor, but because he was a thief; he kept the common purse and used to steal what was put into it" (John 12:6).

Subsequently, John has Jesus issue the same sort of rebuke as in Mark.

> Leave her alone. She bought it so that she might keep it for the day of my burial. *You always have the poor with you, but you do not always have me.*" (John 12:7–8, emphasis added)

John uses the same basic phrase that Mark uses about the poor. But he amends the passage slightly. He notes that the woman actually bought the ointment, suggesting that she was wealthy. And he also indicates that she did not use all of the ointment but that she was saving some of it for the day of burial.

Synoptic Parallels

John's story has points of contact with each of the three Synoptic Gospels. Only Matthew and John say disciples were involved in the criticism. Only Luke and John have the anointing on the feet instead of the head, both also break the chronological connection between the anointing and the betrayal by Judas and both appear to place the story somewhere other than the house of Simon the leper, although Luke keeps the "Simon" portion of the name. Only Mark and John say that the oil was made of nard and cost 300 denarii.

It is easy to see from these parallels how one might argue that John knew all three Synoptic Gospels and made changes as he needed for his own purposes. Reading Mark and John together we can discern a basic story underlying the four versions.

In Bethany, in the home of a man suffering from (or having suffered from) a disease or illness (Simon the leper or Lazarus), shortly before the arrest of Jesus, a woman bought an expensive oil made of nard worth about three hundred denarii. She poured the oil on Jesus and one or more people present (possibly one or more disciples) complained that it would have been better to give the money to the poor. Jesus then defended the woman's actions and said "For you always have the poor with you, and you can show kindness to them whenever you wish; but you will not always have me." Jesus indicated that some portion of the oil was for his burial.

From this basic story we can look at the divergences and see what they suggest about the source material.

The Complainers

There are two key problems here.

1. Why does Matthew, who uses Mark as a source, change Mark's vague "some" to a more specific "disciples"?
2. If John knew any of the three Synoptic Gospels, let alone all three, why would he change the story so that the chief critic of Jesus, in a story that may be somewhat embarrassing to early Christians, is Judas, the one who allegedly betrayed him?

John not only makes Judas the critic, he adds a gloss absent from the other Gospels indicating that Judas was motivated by greed rather than kindness towards the poor. The gloss emphasizes the embarrassing nature of the critique leveled at Jesus. Either Judas was the original complainer in the story or John saw an opportunity to undermine the criticism by placing the unpopular Judas in the role of critic and accusing him of base motives.

That Matthew identifies the disciples as the complainers suggests that at the very least if Judas wasn't the original complainer than perhaps the disciples as a group were. If that were the case, it might have simplified John's task in narrowing the criticism down to a single unpopular disciple.

On the other hand, if the disciples were the complainers why does Mark use the vague "some" instead of directly citing the disciples? And, if Mark did use "some" why did Matthew, who used Mark as a source, choose to say "disciples" instead of leaving Mark's vague terminology in place? Mark may have known the story with disciples and felt uncomfortable with the direct criticism from Jesus' closest followers and made the change. Matthew simply stuck to the story as he knew it. However, perhaps Mark originally referred to the "disciples" as the complainers and Matthew followed Mark's text as he had it. If that were the case it would suggest that a later scribe, copying Mark's Gospel, felt embarrassed by the identification and altered it in a way that came to be version that survived in transmission.

How one might resolve this issue will, no doubt, be influenced by one's other theories about the nature of the Gospels and their development.

Parallel Divergences from Mark

An interesting feature of Luke's departures from Mark is that they appear to be paralleled in John. Luke and John change Mark's location from the house of Simon the Leper in Bethany to a different location and both have a different identity as to the host (although John keeps the city of Bethany as the setting and Luke keeps part of Simon's name as one of the hosts). Luke and John both break Mark's chronological link to Judas's meeting with the priests immediately after the anointing incident. Luke and John both change the pouring of the oil from Jesus' head to Jesus' feet. It could also be argued that both Luke and John attribute base motives to the complainers, a factor not present in Mark or Matthew.

These many parallels between Luke and John in a single story, absent in Mark and Matthew, suggest some sort of commonality between them. The unresolved issue is whether either Luke or John copied from the other or both knew a similar story. At the same time, both Luke and John have very different settings for the story, both of which vary from Mark and Matthew. The different settings in Luke and John might seem like an argument against the one copying from the other, but at the same time Luke diverges significantly from Mark's setting, too, and he very likely had Mark as a source. So a substantial change in setting doesn't always mean a lack of copying.

A look at the story of the anointing in Bethany showed some evidence of overlap between the Gospel of John and each of the Synoptic Gospels. However, the link between John and Matthew is very weak. Matthew says "disciples" complained while John says "Judas," whom he identifies as a disciple, If John altered a previous story it is not clear that he was altering a story where the complainers were "disciples" as opposed to a vague "some." His substitution of Judas could have been for reasons unrelated to his being a disciple. This leaves significant factual correlations between John and Mark and between John and Luke.

Shared details with Mark, such as the nature of the oil and its price, offer some evidence that John either used Mark or both knew a common written or oral source for the story. Taking the story in isolation, it is difficult to determine which option is more likely.

As to the similarities between Luke and John, based on this story and several other common elements in other stories, there appears to be a good case of some sort or literary connection between these two Gospels. Either they shared a common source or one knew the other. On the other hand, while there is a similarity in some of the story elements, they are more thematic than verbal. They tell very different stories and the details of their areas of agreement are often factually at odds.

One problem with positing a literary connection between John and any of the other Gospels, at least in connection with the anointing story, is that only John makes Judas the one who complained about Jesus neglecting the poor. Either he had some reason to substitute Judas for an unidentified critic in all of the other Gospels, perhaps to diminish the credibility of the accusation, or Judas was the original critic and Mark changed the story to hide his identity in order to avoid the embarrassment of having such a critic accuse Jesus of inappropriate conduct.

The Gospel accounts of the Anointing at Bethany provide a good illustration of why scholars continue to debate whether the author of John knew any of the Synoptic Gospels and, if so, which ones he knew.

Evidence for Sequential Agreement between John and Mark

In our examination of the literary relationship among the Synoptic Gospels we looked chiefly at two major issues, sequential agreement and verbal agreement. One of the key differences between John and the Synoptics is the substantial lack of verbal agreement. We find from time to time, such as in the anointing story above, that John sometimes knows or shares some factual details with one Gospel or another but the verbal setting is very often nothing at all like the Synoptic Gospels. The stories often have significant plot variations or appear in a form that is almost unrecognizable. Outside of a quote from Jesus, which may be well-known, there is often little agreement on the phrases or unusual words that make up the story.

Because there were many stories about Jesus circulating in oral and perhaps written fashion prior to the writing of any of the Gospels, it wouldn't be surprising that some particular stories were better known than others and that certain story elements were commonly known. This could account for the occasional agreement on unusual factual details, such as "300 denarii" or "oil of nard." But what are we to make of a situation where we have a lengthy sequence of several stories in John that appear in the same narrative order in Mark but that, in many instances are unalike or hard to recognize in the form that John gives. Raymond Brown argues that "[t]hose who advocate dependence have to agree that John used Mark in a way very different from the way Matthew and Luke drew upon Mark."[106]

In this section we will take a close look at John 5–6, which I have broken down into thirteen separate story units. Every one of these story units has a counterpart in Mark, and almost every one of counterparts appears in the same sequential order that John has. In the few cases where there is some differences in the order of the story units the differences are mostly trivial and reflect some intentional reworking by either John or Mark. Table 3.1 provides an outline of the story units that I will be working with.

Structural Overview of Table 3.1

I have divided John 5–6 into thirteen story units. I treat all of John 5, which is a lengthy story about a Sabbath healing conflict in Jerusalem, as a single story unit. The other twelve story units all occur in John 6. I have further subdivided John 5–6 into four major consecutive literary units, each encompassing a group of story units, such that each of the thirteen story units appear in one of the larger literary units. The case for dividing the sequence into four larger groups comes from verbal clues and settings in John coupled with breaks in Mark at the corresponding points in the narrative. I will examine these break points further below. For purposes of convenience I have given each of the four larger units a name. The groupings are as follows:

1. The Sabbath Healing unit (John 5–6:3; Mark 3:1–14);
2. The Bread and Water unit (John 6:4–29; Mark 6:34–52, 8:27–28);
3. The Bread Metaphor unit. (John 6:30–59; Mark 6:1–6, 8:11–21, 34–38);
4. The Jesus Identity unit (John 6:60–71; Mark 8:29–33).

In the course of the following discussion, when I refer to a *story* unit I am referring to one of the thirteen numbered units in Table 3.1; when I refer to a *literary* unit I am referring to one of the four literary subdivisions in Table 3.1.

The order of the thirteen story units is the one that is followed in John 5–6. The order in John is slightly different from that in Mark, but not in any significant way that undermines the analysis. The most significant deviations are in story units 4 and 9. John's fourth story unit, about the crowd identifying Jesus as a special form of prophet, appears to be out of sequence with Mark's similar story unit. I believe that John moved the unit into the earlier section for reasons to be stated further below. The

TABLE 3.1 Sequential Comparison of John 5–6 to Mark			
Incident Description	*John*	*Mark-A*	*Mark-B*
The Sabbath Healing Unit			
1. Sabbath Healing Violation Jesus heals an invalid on the Sabbath Authorities object Jesus makes an argument in defense of actions Plot to Kill Jesus	John 5	Mark 3:1–6	
2. Jesus at the Sea of Galilee Jesus crosses (flees across?) Sea of Galilee Crowd hails him for miraculous healings Jesus goes up on a mountain with his disciples	John 6:1–3	Mark 3:7–14	
The Bread and Water Unit "Now the Passover, the festival of the Jews, was near (John 6:4)." Language suggests the start of a new literary unit.			
3. Miracle of the Loaves	John 6:5–13 5000 people 12 baskets 5 loaves 2 fish 200 denarii	Mark 6:34–44 5000 people 12 baskets 5 loaves 2 fish 200 denarii	Mark 8:1–9 4000 people 7 baskets 7 loaves A few fish
4. Crowd identifies Jesus as a special prophet	John 6:15	Mark 8:27–28	Mark 8:27–28
5. Jesus walks on Water Jesus goes up on a mountain Disciples get in a boat and head across sea Jesus walks on water alongside boat Disciples terrified	John 16–24	Mark 6:45–51	Mark 8:10 Jesus and disciples get in boat. No miracle.

Continued

TABLE 3.1 Continued

Incident Description	John	Mark-A	Mark-B
6. Followers fail to understand the true meaning of the miracle of the loaves	John 6:25–29	Mark 6:52 Also Mark 8:16–17	Mark 8:16–17

The Bread Metaphor Unit

Incident Description	John	Mark-A	Mark-B
7. Jews ask for a sign/ Jesus declines to give one	John 6:30–34	Mark 8:11–13	Mark 8:11–13
8. Jesus uses a "bread" metaphor and teaches about the multiplication of the loaves	John 6:35–40	Mark 8:14:21	Mark 8:14–21
9. Jews offended by Jesus' teaching. Refer to Jesus' family members.	John 6:41–42	Mark 6:1–6	Not in Mark-B
10. Teachings about obtaining eternal life	John 6:43–58	Mark 8:34–38	Mark 8:34–38

"He said these things while he was teaching in the synagogue at Capernaum. (John 6:59)." Language suggests the end of a literary unit.

The Jesus Identity Unit

Incident Description	John	Mark-A	Mark-B
11. Disciples have a hard time with Jesus' teachings. Offended by claim that he will rise from the dead.	John 6:60–66	Mark 8:31–32	Mark 8:31–32
12. Peter confesses Jesus	John 6:67–69	Mark 8:29–30	Mark 8:29–30
13. Jesus says one of the disciples is Satan	John 6:70-71	Mark 8:33	Mark 8:33

ninth story unit, referencing Jesus' family, corresponds to a similar incident in Mark but John may have inserted this unit into the larger sequence and it may not have originally belonged in this set of four literary units. This, too, will be discussed further below.

If Mark was the original source for John 5–6, then Mark has the original sequential order and John has altered it. If John didn't know

Mark but both relied on a common written source, then we have a more difficult time in determining the original order of the stories. If the correspondences between John and Mark are coincidental, then there is probably no original order to the stories.

As a general rule scholars tend to treat John 5 and John 6 in isolation from each other. John 5 takes place in Jerusalem. John 6 abruptly shifts the center of action to Galilee. This abrupt geographic and chronological shift has led many scholars to believe that John has altered the order of the original narrative. Brown, for example, observes that geographically John 6 works better before John 5 than after.[107] But, he argues, the Evangelist may have deliberately chosen this arrangement for thematic reasons. Brown observes that John 6 deals with a "bread" theme and John 7:37–38 contains a water theme and the Evangelist may have intended to echo the Exodus story, where God provides bread from heaven and water from a rock.[108] Implicit in his arguments is that John 5 and 6 do not belong together as a literary unit.

In the course of the analysis below I will suggests that John 5 belongs with John 6:1–3 and that this grouping originally constituted an independent literary unit separate and apart from the rest of John 6. Together, John 5 and John 6:1–3 form the first literary division in this study, The Sabbath Healing unit.

Mark-A versus Mark-B

If you look at Table 3.1 you will notice that I have two different verse sequences for Mark, one labeled Mark-A, the other Mark-B. The chief difference between Mark-A and Mark-B concerns the second major division in our study, the Bread and Water unit. For the Third and Fourth literary units, Mark-A and Mark-B are identical.

To avoid confusion, let me explain why I have a Mark-A and Mark-B. For reasons explained just below, I believe Mark had two separate versions of the second literary unit, the Bread and Water sequence, with significant factual differences between the two. (See Table 3.1 for the different numbers in Mark's two feeding miracles.) Because of the differences Mark believed they described separate incidents in Jesus' life and included both sets of stories in his Gospels. For editorial and perhaps theological reasons I suggest he rearranged the material from both sources. It is my belief, not necessarily endorsed by most scholars, that the second literary unit in Mark-A was originally attached to the third literary unit in Mark-A and that Mark detached them, moving the second literary unit to an earlier position in the Gospel. He then inserted part of Mark-B into the position where Mark-A's second literary unit was located and the rest of Mark-B into another location in the Gospel. Whether or not my analysis is correct, Mark-A still contains the same four literary units as John and in the same order. Let's take a brief closer look at Mark-A and Mark-B.

The Bread and Water unit consists of two major story units involving miracles and two lesser story units related to the miracle stories. The two miracle stories tell about Jesus multiplying five loaves of bread to feed 5000 people and Jesus walking on water. Despite some minor differences in the story details, John and Mark-A have a very close narrative fit in this unit. The problem is that Mark has a second story about Jesus multiplying loaves of bread to feed a large crowd and the numbers are very different from the ones used in John and Mark-A.

In John and Mark-A, after the feeding miracle Jesus goes up on a mountain and the disciples get in a boat and cross the sea. While the disciples are at sea, Jesus walks across the water and joins them. In Mark -B, Jesus does not go up on the mountain but rather gets in the boat with the disciples. However, Mark-B also omits the walking on water miracle.

A secondary complication is that Mark also has a second miracle out on the water but separate and apart from this sequence. At Mark 4:35–41 we are told that Jesus and the disciples were in a boat and a storm arose. The disciples panicked but Jesus calmed the storm and then chastised them for their lack of faith. While the two water miracles are different in content, they are similar in theme, miraculous intervention while crossing the sea.

I think it is reasonable to argue that this miracle on the water story originally belonged with the second feeding story in Mark-B and that Mark, for editorial reasons may have moved it to another location in his Gospel. If that were the case then a further argument could be made that the second literary unit in Mark-A originally belonged where he placed Mark-B and that Mark switched the pieces around in order to accommodate the two feeding story units. That would mean that originally Mark 8 encompassed all of the last three literary units in a tight narrative, much the way that John 6 does, further strengthening the case that there is some sort of literary connection between John 6 and Mark 8. That conclusion, however, requires us to rely heavily on speculation. So I include it here for the purposes of examining the full range of the evidence. For the balance of the analysis I will just use Mark-A.

The Passover and Eucharist Problem

John 6:4 introduces a Passover theme into his narrative. "Now the Passover, the festival of the Jews, was near." This begins the second literary section, the Bread and Water unit. This unit consists primarily of a Bread miracle and a Water miracle. As noted above in a quote from Raymond Brown, Bread and Water miracles both play lifesaving roles in the Exodus story, the subject of the Passover festival. Bread came in the form of "manna" from heaven and water came out of a rock when Moses struck it. However, the Exodus story of Passover also includes a miraculous intervention when the Israelites crossed the sea. In this particular literary unit the water miracle recalls not the water from the rock but the miraculous intervention while crossing the sea. So John's binding of Bread and Water miracles together serves his Passover theme and also provides a springboard for the Bread Metaphor unit in John, where Jesus delivers a discourse on the Bread of Life theme.

John's Bread of Life teaching presents a form of the Eucharistic teaching, in which Jesus equates himself with "bread" and argues that it is necessary to eat this bread to obtain eternal life. The location of this discourse suggests some chronological and sequential manipulation on John's part.

Mark also has a teaching about bread being the body of Jesus (Mark 14:22). But in Mark this teaching takes place at the Last Supper just before Jesus is arrested, and Mark has no clear explanation as to what it means to eat this bread/body. John's account of the last supper omits this Eucharistic teaching and his Gospel places it within this Bread Metaphor unit, and includes an extended lecture on what it means to eat the bread/body of Jesus. We need, therefore, to resolve the issue of whether the Eucharist teaching better belongs early in the mission with John 6 or at the end of the mission with Mark 14.

The most important evidence on this issue comes from Paul's first letter to the Corinthians. Paul makes the following claim.

> For I received from the Lord what I also handed on to you, that the Lord Jesus on the night when he was betrayed took a loaf of bread, and when he had given thanks, he broke it and said, "This is my body that is for you. Do this in remembrance of me." (1 Cor 11:23–24)

Paul says here that the Eucharistic teaching came to him as a revelation which he passed on to the Corinthians. He clearly places it at the Last Supper. By saying that this teaching came to him through a revelation from the deceased Jesus, Paul implies that he originated the institution of the Eucharist. That may or may not be the case, depending upon what other Apostles who were present at the Last Supper may have taught. However, it would appear that Mark more closely reflects the Eucharist chronology according to Paul than does John. Paul's letter suggests that John has taken an earlier story about a bread metaphor, such as the one in Mark's Bread Metaphor unit, and transformed it into the Bread of Life discourse by substituting the later Eucharist teaching for the earlier bread metaphor.

The Hometown Rejection Problem

Above I mentioned that story unit 9, which appears in the middle of John's Bread Metaphor unit, creates a chronological problem with respect to Mark's story order. It seems to implicitly draw on another story from Mark that doesn't fit into Mark's sequence of stories. In story unit 9 John portrays the Jews complaining about the teachings of Jesus.

> Then the Jews began to complain about him because he said, "I am the bread that came down from heaven." They were saying, "*Is not this Jesus, the son of Joseph, whose father and mother we know?* How can he now say, 'I have come down from heaven'?" (John 6:41–42, emphasis added)

This portion of John's narrative appears to parallel a separate incident recorded in Mark 6:1–6. According to that account Jesus went to his "hometown" and delivered a lecture in the synagogue. The congregation was apparently offended by the teaching and they remark,

> "Is not this the carpenter, the son of Mary and brother of James and Joses and Judas and Simon, and are not his sisters here with us? (Mark 6:3)

Jesus responds, "Prophets are not without honor, except in their hometown, and among their own kin, and in their own house" (Mark 6:4).

John's story has several points of contact with Mark's story.

First, with the reference to Jesus' family, John and Mark have different versions of the family quote. John talks about Jesus' father and mother and gives the father's name as Joseph. Mark talks about everyone other than the father. Initially, this would seem to indicate a lack of connection between the two family passages, but other evidence reinforces the link.

In some ancient sources Mark's passage reads "*son of* the carpenter."[109] In Matthew, the corresponding passage uses the phrase, "Is not this the carpenter's son?" (Matt 13:55); in Luke, the corresponding passage includes the statement, "Is not this Joseph's son?" (Luke 4:22). So Matthew and Luke, who used Mark as a source, both refer to the father. This latter point is particularly interesting as both Matthew and Luke are the only two Gospels to tell us that Jesus was born of a virgin mother. For these reasons, some scholars argue that "son of the carpenter" is the original form for Mark 6:3 and that later a scribe must have edited the passage to eliminate the reference to Jesus' human father.[110]

Of particular interest, Luke actually gives the father's name as Joseph, just as John does. This, of course, raises the further question of whether Luke or John knew the other's Gospel or a common source in which the father's name was actually used for this incident. It also suggests that several versions of the story were well-known. That Luke also uses the name of Jesus' father clearly connects John's passage to a version of Mark's synagogue rejection story.

Second, John's familiarity with the underlying story is evidenced by his claim at another place in his Gospel, outside of the John 5–6 sequence, that "Jesus himself had testified that a prophet has no honor in the prophet's own country" (John 4:44). John is paraphrasing Jesus here, not quoting him precisely, which suggests that he (or his source) was aware of the story tradition but not fully certain of the exact quote. That in turn suggests an oral source for the story rather than a written source. John has divided the synagogue rejection story into two parts, one part being inserted into the Bread of Life discourse, the other being placed elsewhere in a different context.

A third point of contact between John's phrase and Mark's story is the location. John says that Jesus gave this teaching at Capernaum (John 6:59). Mark just says that he gave the lecture in his "hometown" without specifying the location. The problem is that Mark is vague about the location and that either Capernaum or near-by Nazareth could be the hometown.

Mark and Matthew both indicate that Jesus moved his operation from his alleged childhood home of Nazareth to nearby Capernaum very early in his mission.[111] Mark places the move prior to the call of most of the disciples (Mark 2:1). According to Matthew Jesus "left Nazareth and made his home in Capernaum" and also places the move prior to the call of the twelve disciples (Matt 4:13). Luke, on the other hand, is the only Gospel specifically placing the synagogue incident in Nazareth. Mark may have been vague because he did not know if the incident happened in Nazareth or Capernaum. Further, that the community in John's story knows the family of Jesus shows that the underlying story takes place in

Jesus' hometown, wherever it may be. These details further suggest that the story was generally well-know but circulated only in oral form with inconsistent details.

A fourth point of contact with Mark's story is that the quote is placed in the context of a teaching that is hostilely received by the Jewish audience.

If John specifically knew the Gospel of Mark it seems odd that he would so alter Mark's reference to the family of Jesus such that he names and emphasizes the one person whose name is clearly omitted from Mark (in either version of Mark's passage). At the same time he has a different version of the "prophet without honor" quote than Mark has, omitting the reference to Mark's kin. The inconsistency here between John and Mark is one of those situations that raises doubts as to whether John knew Mark.

In either event, we see that John has taken a story and divided it up into separate pieces, placing one part outside of John 6. This raises a question as to whether the underlying story was originally part of the "Bread Metaphor" unit, as John has it, or was separate from the unit as Mark has it. We'll discuss this issue further when we consider this issue below.

"The Sabbath Healing" Unit (John 5–6:3; Mark 3:1–14)

John 5 tells of a conflict in Jerusalem in which Jewish authorities accuse Jesus of violating the Sabbath laws by healing an invalid on the Sabbath and having him lift his mat and carry it away (John 5:8). In the course of the confrontation with the authorities Jesus makes an argument in support of his actions. "My Father is still working, and I also am working" (John 5:17). Despite Jesus' response the authorities threaten Jesus with death (John 5:18).

This story does not appear in Mark, at least in the form of a Sabbath violation. It could be argued that the incident in John is loosely based on Mark's non-Sabbath story of the healing of the paralytic (Mark 2:1–12) and John simply threw in a claim that the event happened on the Sabbath (John 5:9), but I won't be making that argument at this time. Mark does, however, have a Sabbath violation story in which Jesus cures a man with a withered hand, is accused of violating the Sabbath, makes an argument in defense of his actions, and the authorities seek to put Jesus to death (Mark 3:1–6).

Mark's story does not appear in John and a good case can be and frequently has been made that Mark's story, without any specific act of labor involved in the cure, fails to show that any Sabbath violation took place according to Jewish practices. It may be that John (or his source) reached a similar conclusion about the original story and used a different Sabbath incident so that the alleged Sabbath violation becomes much more explicit. (The direction to lift the mat and carry it away provides the necessary act of labor that indicates a Sabbath violation may have occurred according to Jewish law.)

For purposes of our analysis I am going to start the narrative sequences in John and Mark with the Sabbath violation stories in Mark 3:1–6 and John 5. Admittedly, they are different stories in terms of the specific events that take place, but, plot-wise they are similar. The two stories constitute the only incident in each Gospel where Jesus heals an invalid on the Sabbath, Jesus gets accused of a Sabbath violation, and Jews threaten to kill Jesus for the violation. John 9 also has a story in which Jesus also heals a blind man on the Sabbath and arouses Jewish anger, but this infirmity is of a different nature than the two crippling injuries in question.

Immediately after the Sabbath stories in both John and Mark, Jesus crosses the Sea of Galilee and is met by a large crowd that heard about his miraculous healings (John 6:1–2; Mark 3:7–11). The juxtaposition of the crowd hailing Jesus for healing immediately after an incident in which Jesus healed somebody strongly suggests that the greeting event is closely related to the healing incident. While not specifically mentioned in either Gospel, crossing the Sea of Galilee immediately after receiving a death threat suggests that in the original version of the story the journey may have been presented as an escape from the threatening local authorities. After being hailed by the crowd, Jesus goes up on a mountain with his disciples (John 6:3; Mark 3:13–14).

At this point John inserts a claim that the Jewish Passover was near (John 6:4). John's reference to the coming Passover suggests a narrative transition from what has just occurred and indicates that what follows was originally a separate literary unit from what preceded it. In theory, John's transition here could indicate an undocumented chronological jump to a later point in time. Implicitly, there should be a chronological break because the John 5 Sabbath story in Jerusalem took place at a "festival of the Jews" (John 5:1). So if Passover is near, some period of time must have passed after the Jerusalem events to allow for a transition from one Jewish festival period to another.

At this same point where John introduces the upcoming Passover reference, Mark jumps to a later location in his Gospel before we resume the narrative parallel between John and Mark. This seems to reinforce the idea that the Passover reference is a literary marker separating what comes before from what comes after, indicating that the preceding passage is a separate literary unit.

To summarize: John 5–6:3 and Mark 3:1–14 share the following sequence of events in the exact same order without disruption.

- The only instance in each Gospel where Jesus heals a crippling infirmity on the Sabbath;
- Jesus engages in an argument over whether he violated the Sabbath;
- Authorities plot to kill Jesus for this alleged violation;
- Jesus immediately crosses (or escapes across) the Sea of Galilee;
- A large crowd that heard about Jesus' miraculous healings greets him;
- Jesus goes up on a mountain with his disciples;
- John introduces a scene-shifting passage about Passover and Mark's narrative parallel breaks off.

As I indicated above, scholars tend to separate John 5 from John 6 in their analysis. Many consider the stories out of order and geographically inconsistent. But, given that Mark 3:7–14 follows immediately after his Sabbath violation story and the events described parallel almost exactly the same events that follow immediately after John's Sabbath violation story, and that the events are thematically related to healing, strongly suggests that there existed some form of literary unit in which there existed a Sabbath healing story that generated a death threat from authorities followed by a trip (escape?) across the Galilee, crowd recognition for the miraculous event, and a private meeting between Jesus and his disciples on a mountain (perhaps to discuss the meaning of what has occurred.) It may be that the Sabbath portion of the story in its original form was not very detailed—Mark's only takes up six verses—and allowed both Gospel authors considerable latitude to frame their own versions. I also suggested above that if John or his source knew Mark's story (or a source for Mark's story) they may have found it insufficiently convincing as a Sabbath violation story and substituted a different violation incident to enhance the narrative.

Given that both John and Mark seem to break off the literary unit at this point suggests that it may have been self-contained and not necessarily part of a larger narrative. As such, given its brevity in Mark, a solely oral transmission of the story would not be out of the question. On the other hand, the author of John could have known Mark and may have adapted it to his own purposes. It's less likely that the author of John could have used Matthew or Luke since neither follows the full sequence in close order the way Mark does. Matthew is missing both the trip across the sea and the meeting on the mountain (Matt 12:9–17) and Luke not only lacks the crossing of the sea but he also has the crowd and the mountain meeting in a reverse order from Mark and John (Luke 6:6–19).

"The Bread and Water" Unit (John 6:4–29; Mark 6:34–52)

John's narrative continues with the story of the Feeding of the Five Thousand (John 6:4–14). The same story appears in Mark 6:34–44. Both stories agree that there were five loaves of bread, 2 fish, a potential expenditure of 200 denarii, scraps were gathered in 12 baskets, and there were five thousand people fed. The two narratives contain some factual variations but nothing that can't be explained by some editorial tinkering.

In both John and Mark, immediately after the feeding of the 5,000, the Gospels say that Jesus went up on a mountain and the disciples got into a boat to cross the sea (John 6:15–16; Mark 6:45–46). Despite this agreement between John and Mark about Jesus going up on a mountain, the two Gospels disagree as to why Jesus went up on the mountain. In Mark Jesus went up to pray (Mark 6:46). In John, Jesus went on the mountain to escape the crowds that wanted to force him to become king (John 6:15).

John's explanation for why Jesus went up on the mountain introduces a small break in Mark's sequential narrative agreement. Mark's sequential order has no corresponding reference to the public reaction to Jesus at this point in the narrative, but he does have a parallel in what appears to belong to the "Jesus Identity" unit.

In John 6:15, "When Jesus realized that they were about to come and take him by force to make him king, he withdrew again to the mountain by himself." At Mark 8:27 Jesus asks the disciples, "Who do people say that I am?" They respond, "John the Baptist; and others, Elijah; and still others, one of the prophets." Despite the difference in how the crowd perceives Jesus' special status, the stories appear to be parallel incidents. In both John and Mark we are dealing with the issue of how the public perceives Jesus and Jesus' negative reaction to what the respective authors see as a mistake in understanding Jesus' true nature.

This incident constitutes story unit 4, and as I said above, this is one of the places where there is a significant variation between Mark and John in the narrative order. Mark's passage is part of the larger story in his Jesus Identity unit. That John's placement seems to be somewhat out of order is suggested by the fact that in his narrative, after Jesus escapes from the crowd that wants to force him to be king, the same crowd follows after him when he crosses the sea and makes no further note of their desire that he be king (John 6:24–25). For purposes of correspondence I have placed Mark 8:27–28 alongside of John 6:15. Further below I will suggest that story unit 4 originally belonged with the Jesus Identity literary unit and that John has shifted it into the second literary unit for theological reasons.

In both John and Mark after Jesus goes up on the mountain the disciples depart in a boat. In Mark the disciples leave during the day, in John they wait until evening. This notice serves as a prelude to Jesus walking on the water (John 6:18–21; Mark 6:47–51). Both Gospels describe the disciples as terrified by Jesus' appearance. Once they realize that it was Jesus walking on the water both Gospels say that the disciples tried to take him into the boat. In John, when the disciples do so the boat miraculously appears on the opposite shore. In Mark, Jesus gets in the boat and sails across the sea with them. The story is broadly the same but some of the details differ. John 6:22–24 adds a little additional detail to the "walking on water" story that is missing from Mark. It says that the crowd on the original side of the sea wonders how Jesus disappeared and they seek after him across the water in Capernaum.

In Mark, right after Jesus gets in the boat, we are told that "the wind ceased. And they were utterly astounded, for they did not understand about the loaves, but their hearts were hardened" (Mark 6:52). This is truly an odd statement. It lacks context. Mark doesn't explain at this point why the disciples were upset or why their hearts hardened. But the passage suggests that the disciples had some sort of negative reaction to an undisclosed teaching.

In John, the context is cleaner. It is not the disciples who don't understand; it is the crowd that approaches Jesus when he gets off the boat. "Very truly, I tell you, you are looking for me, not because you saw signs, but because you ate your fill of the loaves" (John 6:26). Jesus has to explain to them that they failed to understand the signs associated with the feeding. So both John and Mark come to a point where the message of the loaves is not understood but there is some disagreement over who did not understand the message.

John 6:4:29 and Mark 6:34–52 share the following parallels in the same uninterrupted sequential order.

- Jesus feeds the five thousand, and the several numerical details in both stories are the same;
- Jesus goes up on a mountain;
- Disciples get in a boat;
- Jesus walks on water;

- The disciples are terrified;
- The miracle of the loaves is misunderstood.

In addition there is one story element out of sequential order. John places the public perception of Jesus as a special "human" leader in this section; Mark puts it in the Jesus Identity unit.

The "Bread Metaphor" Unit (John 6:30–59; Mark 6:1–6, 8:11–21)

The separation between the second and third unit is not explicit and it is not entirely clear that an actual break existed in the source material. There are indications within both John and Mark that aspects of the third unit refer back to the second unit.

John begins the unit with the crowd requesting a sign so that they can believe in his powers (John 6:30). This is an odd request in the narrative sequence and one reason to think the third literary unit may have originally existed independently of the second. The people asking for a sign here appear to be the same people who witnessed and participated in the miracle of the multiplication of the loaves. Just a couple of verses earlier, Jesus says, "you are looking for me, not because you saw signs, but because you ate your fill of the loaves" (John 6:26).

So they already had evidence of Jesus' miraculous power. In John, Jesus chastises them for failing to appreciate the signs they saw. So why would the same crowd that witnessed the miracle and discussed it with Jesus ask for some sort of sign of Jesus' powers as if they had not seen such a sign. This suggests that there may be an undocumented shift in the scene such that the crowd that Jesus addresses now differs from the crowd he previously addressed in the second unit. Mark 8:11 reinforces that idea. In his version of the request for a sign the people asking were not witnesses to what occurred with the loaves of bread. So while the starting point may not be precisely defined, there is good reason to think that the request for a sign signifies a change of scene before a different audience, which in turn suggests the start of a new literary unit.

While we have no clear literary marker indicating a divider between the second and third literary units, we do have a good indication as to where this third unit in John should end and the fourth unit begin. The central feature of the third unit in John is Jesus' "Bread of Life" discourse. At the end of his teaching we are told that "He said these things while he was teaching in the synagogue at Capernaum" (John 6:59). The statement strongly suggests that we have come to the end of a literary unit and are about to begin a new unit.

In Mark, the division between the third and fourth units is imprecise. In theory, we would expect Mark 8:11–21 to constitute the third unit and Mark 8:27–33 to encompass the fourth unit. In between those two sections we have the one story in Mark 8 that doesn't appear in John 6, the story of Jesus healing a blind man.[112] In Mark, therefore, the two story units are separated.

The problem occurs with Mark 8:34–38. In this section Jesus delivers a teaching that following him is the way to eternal life. John also has a teaching connecting himself to the quest for eternal life but that teaching takes place during John's third literary unit. The question here is whether Mark moved the "eternal life" teaching from the third literary unit and placed it after the fourth, or did John move the "eternal life" teaching from the end of the fourth literary unit and integrate it into the third unit as part of his Eucharist teaching. This is another question that will have to remain open.

Request for a Sign

John 6:30–31, the passage which begins this unit in the Johannine narrative sequence, has the Jews in the crowd asking for a sign. "So they said to him, 'What sign are you going to give us then, so that we may see it and believe you? What work are you performing?'" The Jews add an observation about God having given the Jews "bread from heaven" when they wandered in the desert during the Exodus. The Exodus reference incorporates the Passover theme into the story and gives Jesus an opening to move into the Bread of Life teaching.

In Mark 8:11, which begins the third unit in that Gospel, we also have Jews asking Jesus for a sign. "The Pharisees came and began to argue with him, asking him for a sign from heaven, to test him." In Mark 8:12 Jesus denounces the Jews for asking for a sign. "Why does this generation ask for a sign? Truly I tell you, no sign will be given to this generation." While Mark's Jesus specifically chastises the crowd for asking for a sign, John's Jesus is less hostile, criticizing them for not understanding where signs come from. "Very truly, I tell you, it was not Moses who gave you the bread from heaven, but it is my Father who gives you the true bread from heaven" (John 6:32–34).

The Bread of Life Discourse

When John finishes the dialogue over the request for a sign, he has Jesus deliver the Bread of Life discourse. Similarly, in Mark, after the dialogue over the request for a sign Jesus makes use of a "bread" metaphor, but on the surface it appears to be quite different than John's. Digging a little deeper we will find a more substantial parallel.

John's Bread of Life teaching raises an interesting question. Jesus teaches that he is the Bread of Life and that eating the Bread of Life, i.e., Jesus, will give you eternal life (John 6:51). The audience appears to take this in a literal manner and it creates problems with those hearing the message. The Jews then disputed among themselves, saying, "How can this man give us his flesh to eat?" (John 6:51). But was this teaching intended to be taken literally?

In Mark, we also have a bread metaphor. "Watch out—beware of the yeast of the Pharisees and the yeast of Herod" (Mark 8:15). In Mark, this teaching is not understood by the disciples and the disciples ask if it has anything to do with not having bread (Mark 8:16). This leads Jesus to criticize them for not understanding the miracle of the loaves (Mark 8:17). So Mark, like John, has a "bread" metaphor relating back to the miracle of the loaves and, like John's audience, his disciples do not get it.

In Mark, however, it seems quite clear that "bread" is a metaphor for "teaching." In Mark, Jesus uses the metaphor to warn his followers away from other teachings and to try to understand what the miracle of the loaves was all about. But Mark doesn't actually have an explanation for what the miracle means. "Do you not yet understand?" (Mark 8:21).

In John, although the context is slightly different, John's Bread of Life should also be understood as a metaphor for "teaching." John's Jesus basically says that if you follow his teaching—i.e., eat Jesus, the Bread of Life—you will have eternal life. In John, the metaphor is used to tell the people what *teachings they should follow* to achieve eternal life; in Mark the disciples are being told what *teachings not to follow* in order to achieve eternal life. In John, the metaphor is more explicitly explained than it is in Mark, but even with John's fuller explanation, the audience, like Mark's disciples, fails to grasp the message. In both John and Mark, then, this unit involves the use of "bread/yeast" as a metaphor for teaching about how to achieve eternal life. Both relate this teaching back to the miracle of the multiplication of the loaves. This miracle has to be understood not merely as the power to physically feed the masses but more importantly as a symbolic message that Jesus offers them "spiritual bread" and they should feed on the "bread/teachings" of Jesus. What teachings they should actually follow to achieve eternal life is a separate question that we won't get into here.

Jews Reject the Teaching

Both Gospels agree on the following sequence of events.

- Jews request a sign from Jesus;
- Jesus declines to give a sign;
- Jesus attempts to explain the miracle of the loaves by using a "bread" metaphor for "teachings" that will lead to eternal life;
- The audience fails to grasp the nature of his teachings.

At this point in John the audience becomes hostile and remarks that they know Jesus' family, the implication being that they knew how he was raised so how did he come up with this offensive teaching (John 6:41–42). We have noted already above that this incident, story unit 9, corresponds to a similar incident in Mark 6:1–6, where Jesus is rejected in his town. Mark's story does not follow John's sequence of events. Mark's account takes place shortly before the miracle of the loaves in Mark 6:33–44. I suspect that John imported the rejection theme from a separate source and inserted it at this location. As suggested earlier John appears to have known the story only in an oral form.

The Eternal Life Teaching (John 6:43–58, Mark 8:34–38)

Following the hostile response from the audience John launches into a speech about how to obtain eternal life by eating his body, the Bread of Life. Mark 8:34–38 also has a teaching by Jesus about obtaining eternal life but it omits the Eucharistic theme of John's discourse. In terms of sequence we don't know if this theme originally appeared in the third literary unit, as in John, or was appended to the fourth literary unit, as in Mark.

In John, the eternal life speech leads to conflict with the followers, which is the subject of the fourth literary unit in John, the "Jesus Identity" unit. While John has a literary marker indicating that the unit has come to an end after this speech (John 6:59) there is no explicit indication that there is any change of scene, audience or locale.

In contrast to John, Mark shows no hostile reaction to the eternal life teaching. Given the lack of a Eucharistic theme that shouldn't be too surprising. Also in contrast to John, Mark's fourth unit also has a distinct break in setting from the third unit. In between the two units Mark records a separate incident about Jesus healing a blind man in the city of Bethsaida. This incident does not appear in John 6 but may have been an inspiration for John's account of a Sabbath healing of a blind man in John 9.

In summary, the third literary unit in both Gospels had the following incidents in the same sequential order.

- Jews ask for a sign;
- Jesus declines to give a sign;
- Use of a "bread" metaphor as a teaching device;
- Teachings about eternal life;

This last entry in Mark, although in the same sequential order within the unit, is separated by other stories in Mark's narrative from the earlier part of the unit. In addition to the stories in sequential order John also referenced a story that seems related to Mark's narrative about Jesus being rejected in his home town. We also saw that John imported the Eucharist teaching from the Last Supper scene and repositioned it in this unit as a substitute for the original "bread" metaphor.

The "Jesus Identity" Unit (John 60–71; Mark 27–33)

We come now to the fourth literary section, the Jesus Identity literary unit, which deals with matters of how Jesus is perceived by others and how the disciples react to his teaching. We should probably insert a word here about the thematic difference between Mark and John about how Jesus is publicly perceived. In Mark, the identity of Jesus as Messiah is never made public; he performs miracles and these are supposed to induce people to draw a conclusion about his true identity, but not even Peter, as we shall see in a moment, gets it right. John, on the other hand posits a Jesus who is constantly telling the public he is working on behalf of the "Father" and how he was sent by the "Father" to do his works. Mark and John have very conflicting views about how Jesus expressed his nature to the public and those different views are evident in the parallel passages in John and Mark.

Mark's Identity Passage (Mark 8:27–33)

It will probably be easier to proceed if we begin with Mark's full passage on identity, and then show how John and Mark share similar broad themes although there is no significant verbal agreement.

> Jesus went on with his disciples to the villages of Caesarea Philippi; and on the way he asked his disciples, "Who do people say that I am?" And they answered him, "John the Baptist; and others, Elijah; and still others, one of the prophets." He asked them, "But who do you say that

I am?" Peter answered him, "You are the Messiah." And he sternly ordered them not to tell anyone about him. Then he began to teach them that the Son of Man must undergo great suffering, and be rejected by the elders, the chief priests, and the scribes, and be killed, and after three days rise again. He said all this quite openly. And Peter took him aside and began to rebuke him. But turning and looking at his disciples, he rebuked Peter and said, "Get behind me, Satan! For you are setting your mind not on divine things but on human things." (Mark 8:27–33)

Mark's passage contains the following elements.
- Discussions of identity and public perception;
- Peter identifies Jesus as the Messiah;
- Jesus teaches about his need to die and rise;
- Peter rebukes Jesus;
- Jesus calls Peter a "Satan";
- Jesus tells Peter he is focused on earthly matters, not heavenly concerns.

We have already noted above that the first element in Mark's story, the public perception of Jesus, has its parallel earlier in John 6:15, when the crowd wants Jesus to be there king.

John's Identity Passage (John 6:60–71)

Let's now look at the corresponding section in John.

When many of his disciples heard it, they said, "This teaching is difficult; who can accept it?" But Jesus, being aware that his disciples were complaining about it, said to them, "Does this offend you? Then what if you were to see the Son of Man ascending to where he was before? It is the spirit that gives life; the flesh is useless. The words that I have spoken to you are spirit and life. But among you there are some who do not believe." For Jesus knew from the first who were the ones that did not believe, and who was the one that would betray him. And he said, "For this reason I have told you that no one can come to me unless it is granted by the Father." Because of this many of his disciples turned back and no longer went about with him. So Jesus asked the twelve, "Do you also wish to go away?" Simon Peter answered him, "Lord, to whom can we go? You have the words of eternal life. We have come to believe and know that you are the Holy One of God." Jesus answered them, "Did I not choose you, the twelve? Yet one of you is a devil." He was speaking of Judas son of Simon Iscariot, for he, though one of the twelve, was going to betray him. (John 6:60–71)

John's account has the following elements.

- A rebuke by disciples (not the Twelve);
- An offending teaching about rising up after death;
- Peter's identification of Jesus;
- Jesus calling a disciple "Satan."

The story elements in John have a different order from those in Mark but it is obviously based on the same fundamental story. The chronological differences reflect editorial tinkering rather than different stories. The chief difference is that John diverts attention away from the conflict between Jesus and Peter. To some extent John has changed the thrust of the public perception story element. We have already noted that his version of that story unit appears earlier in the Gospel. He has replaced it with a crowd of hostile disciples who react negatively to his teachings. The unfolding of this story shows Jesus confronting failure in his mission, wondering if even the Twelve were going to desert him. In Mark, the theme is the same. Jesus is unhappy with the public reaction because it fails to recognize who he really is.

In Mark, when Jesus asks the disciples who they think he is, Peter describes him as "the Messiah." In John, in response to the desertion of his followers, Jesus asks the Twelve if they plan to leave him too. Peter responds, in part, "You have the words of eternal life ... you are the Holy One of God." In both Gospels Peter is praised for his answer, although Mark's Jesus tells Peter not to tell anybody what he said (Mark 8:30). But Mark will quickly reveal that Peter's understanding is deficient while in John it is spot on, reflecting the different perspectives of the two Evangelists.

After Peter's confession in Mark Jesus teaches the disciples that he must die and rise up in three days. This brings on a very negative response by Peter who "rebukes" Jesus for this teaching. John has a similar passage. While confronting his followers who are upset over the Bread of Life teaching, John's Jesus says, in effect, if you think that was offensive what if I were to die and rise up to heaven. This caused many of his followers to desert him. In both Gospels, then, the claim that he will rise from the dead causes consternation among his followers. The chief difference in the two Gospels is that in John, it is those outside of the Twelve who are upset and in Mark it is Peter himself. However, in John those upset are rejecting Jesus while in Mark Peter acts out of love for Jesus and doesn't want to see him suffer.

Nevertheless, Mark says that Jesus took offense at Peter's rebuke, accused him of being a Satan, and declared "For you are setting your mind not on divine things but on human things" (Mark 8:33). In other words, Mark says that Peter didn't truly understand who Jesus was; that he was thinking about an earthly Messiah/king, not a heavenly messiah/king. This brings us full circle to John's having the crowd identify Jesus as an earthly king (John 6:15).

In John, the Evangelist has clearly tried to extricate Peter from the criticism present in Mark. Mark's criticism is that Peter failed to understand who Jesus was because he saw him only as an earthly king. This presented a problem for John, who wanted to place Peter in a positive light. He solved the difficulty by taking the mistaken words about a human king out of Peter's mouth and placing them earlier in the narrative in the mouth of the crowd that failed to understand who Jesus really was after the Bread miracle. Then, after Peter identifies Jesus, John has Jesus say "Did I not choose you, the twelve? Yet one of you is a devil" (John 6:70).

Jesus here doesn't explicitly identify who he is referring to as a devil but John adds a gloss to indicate that Jesus was talking about Judas, who would eventually betray him. It seems highly unlikely that if Jesus originally denounced Judas as the devil that Mark or anyone else would change it from an indirect reference to Judas to a direct reference to Peter. It is most probable that John altered the story to cover up an attack on Peter.

The fourth literary unit consists of a single scene that appears to have been somewhat re-edited by John so the story elements are not in precise chronological order. It includes the following common features in both Gospels.

- Questions about how the public perceives Jesus;
- Questions about how the Twelve perceive Jesus;
- Peter's identification of Jesus' true nature;
- Offense and rebuke over Jesus' teaching about rising up after death;
- The identification of one of the Twelve as a devil.

In addition, it appears that John took the tradition of Peter identifying Jesus as a human king and relocated the mistaken claim by placing it earlier in the narrative and having someone other than Peter make the identification. John also appears to have deflected Jesus' rebuke of Peter by making Judas the target of the attack.

Summary of the Sequential Agreement Between John and Mark

For purposes of analysis I divided John 5–6 into thirteen story units and the evidence suggested that these thirteen story units could be reasonably divided into four larger independent literary units. For all practical purposes Mark and John followed the same schematic arrangement. Of the thirteen story units, Mark had nine counterparts in the same exact order as John. Using the numbering structure in Table 3.1, the stories following the sequential order are numbers 1, 2, 3, 5, 6, 7, 8, 12, and 13. Of the four story units in Mark that don't match John, two (4 and 11) belong to the Jesus Identity unit but John appears to have been the one who changed the story order. This suggests eleven out of thirteen matches. Approximately half of the counterparts in Mark fall into the single chapter, Mark 8.

The two remaining story units in Mark that appear out of sequence include the hometown rejection story (9) and the eternal life discourse (10). The evidence shows that John knew the hometown story unit but probably only in an oral form. He appears to have imported it into his narrative for editorial reasons. This incident was probably not part of the original four main literary units. This leaves only the eternal life discourse in Mark that appears out of sync. Mark places it right after the Jesus Identity unit and John puts it just before that unit. The close proximity of the eternal life story to the fourth unit in both Gospels strongly suggests it was part of the larger narrative collection of story units but we can't clearly say whether Mark or John has the correct sequence here.

We should also recognize that John has taken the Eucharistic teaching from the Last Supper scene, relocated it into the John 6 narrative, combined it with the hometown rejection story, and replaced the original Bread metaphor with the Eucharistic Bread of Life metaphor.

If the author of John knew Mark then there is no problem in explaining the significant amount of sequential agreement. But if John did know Mark why do we have so little additional evidence of substantial sequential agreement in other parts of John and Mark? On the other hand, if John didn't know Mark, then this large number of sequential agreements within tightly defined boundaries in John and Mark suggests the existence of a written source document known by both Evangelists, heavily reworked by John and possibly reworked to a lesser degree by Mark. The likelihood of coincidence in this sequential arrangement seems highly unlikely but not impossible, but it strikes me as the least plausible solution.

For what it's worth, here is what I think happened. John did not know the Gospel of Mark but did know a written source that Mark also knew. This written source had already integrated the four major literary units into a single narrative, representing different chronological stages of Jesus' mission. Both Evangelists incorporated this written source into their own Gospels and made modifications to suit their editorial needs. The discussions above show the sort of changes that John made. Mark, recognizing that this written source presented different stages of Jesus' career, reassigned the first two major literary units to earlier periods in Jesus' mission, thereby retaining the narrative in sequential order.

An unresolved question is whether this earlier written source contained much more than the four literary units discussed here. That discussion will have to await another occasion.

DID JOHN KNOW LUKE?

When we examined the Synoptic Gospels we saw that almost all New Testament scholars believe that Matthew and Luke each copied from Mark. We also saw that Matthew and Luke shared a number of story elements that didn't appear in Mark. This led scholars to wonder if Matthew and Luke shared a common source other than Mark or if the one copied from the other. The vast majority of scholars have postulated that Matthew and Luke shared from a lost common source that they have nicknamed Q. Some have challenged that view by arguing that Luke copied from both Mark and Matthew and that, therefore, no common source is needed to explain the similarities.

A similar problem presents itself with Luke and John. These two Gospels seem to share a number of similarities, mostly with regard to the Passion story, that don't appear in the Gospel of Mark. Either these similarities are a coincidence or there must have been some sort of literary connection between Luke and John. In the latter case that means that either the author of one Gospel copied from the other or the two shared a common source. But if the one copied from the other, why do almost all of the similarities group themselves around the Passion story? Why wouldn't there be more similarities between these two Gospels in the non-Passion areas? This leads some scholars to propose that Luke and John shared a common Passion source that included story elements not present in Mark.

In the balance of this chapter we will look at some of the similarities that suggest to a number of scholars that there is some sort of literary relationship between Luke and John.

Passion Parallels

The primary area of similarity between Luke and John occurs during the Passion narratives. Here are some of the more obvious ones.

- All four Gospels show Jesus being well-received by the crowds when he enters into Jerusalem. But only Luke and John depict the Pharisees as concerned about what is happening. In Luke the Pharisees say, "Teacher, order your disciples to stop" (Luke 19:39). In John, the Pharisees remark, "You see, you can do nothing. Look, the world has gone after him!" (John 12:19). No such reaction occurs in Mark or Matthew.

- Prior to the arrest of Jesus only Luke and John say that Satan entered into Judas and led him to betray Jesus (Luke 23:3; John 13:27). Mark has no motive for Judas's actions and Matthew attributes it to a desire for money.

- After Jesus is arrested Mark says that Jesus was taken to the High Priest, where there was an assembly of elders and scribes gathered (Mark 14:53). Mark doesn't say what sort of facility this meeting took place in and Mark never mentions the High Priest's name. Matthew says that Jesus was taken to the House of the High Priest, where there was an assembly gathered, and Matthew correctly identifies the High Priest as Caiaphas. In John, we are told that Jesus was brought to Annas, "the father-in-law of Caiaphas," was held there overnight without any tribunal assembled, and brought to Caiaphas the next morning (John 18:12–24). John implies that Jesus was brought to the "house" of Annas but doesn't specifically say so. Luke also says that Jesus was brought to the house of the High Priest but doesn't name him at this point. However, Luke appears somewhat confused about the High Priest's identity. At one point early in his Gospel Luke says that John the Baptist received his calling "during the high priesthood of Annas and Caiaphas (Luke 3:2). In Acts 4:6, after the resurrection of Jesus, Luke describes Annas as the High Priest and mentions the presence of Caiaphas only as a member of the priestly family but not the High Priest. Luke appears to have believed that Annas may have been the High Priest or that he shared the position with Caiaphas.

- Both John and Luke omit any mention of an evening tribunal before a Jewish gathering.

- During Mark's night-time proceeding, the High Priest asks Jesus, "Are you the Messiah, the Son of the Blessed One?" (Mark 14:61). A variation on Mark's compound question incorporating two different titles of Jesus (Messiah and Son of the Blessed One) also appears in Matthew, who changes "Blessed One" to "God" (Matt 26:63.) Luke, however, has divided the question into two parts and has the questioning take place on the next morning. First, according to Luke, the High Priest asks, "If you are the Messiah, tell us" (Luke 22:67). In response, Jesus says, "If I tell you, you will not believe" (Luke 22:67). Afterwards, the Priest asks Jesus if he is the Son of God. Compare the first answer and response in Luke with the following interchange in John. "'If you are the Messiah, tell us plainly.' Jesus answered, 'I have told you, and you do not believe'" (John 10:24–25). John and Luke appear to know the same textual unit, but John has placed it in a different setting well before the Passion, at the Festival of Dedication (i.e., Hanukkah).

- In Mark, when Jesus appears before Pilate, the Governor never specifically says that he finds Jesus innocent of the charges. Matthew also has no such specific claim, although he edges closer to the idea by having Pilate wash his hands to show he is not responsible for what is about to happen. In both John and Luke, however, Pilate makes three specific claims that he finds Jesus innocent of the charges (Luke 23:4, 13, 22; John 18:38, 19:4, 6).

- In both John and Luke Pilate expresses a specific concern as to where Jesus comes from, although the two Gospels provide different contexts for the question. In Luke, Pilate asks the Jewish leaders if Jesus comes from Galilee, presumably to shift the proceedings away from himself to Herod (Luke 23:6). In John, Pilate specifically asks Jesus where he comes from but Jesus remains silent. (See the next chapter for problematic issues with this dialogue between Pilate and Jesus.) Herod plays no role in John's Gospel.

- In Mark, it is only after Pilate has decided to have Jesus crucified that the Governor turns Jesus over to his soldiers for flogging and the soldiers mock and abuse Jesus (Mark 15:15–20). In both John and Luke, it is during the proceedings that Pilate hands Jesus over for flogging and the soldiers abuse Jesus. In John, Pilate orders Jesus to be flogged and hands him over to the soldiers, who then mock and abuse him (John 19:1–3). In Luke, there is a slight variation on the scene. Pilate sends Jesus to Herod for further inquiry and it is Herod's soldiers who mock and abuse Jesus (Luke 23:11). When Jesus comes back from Herod Pilate says that he will have Jesus flogged (Luke 23:16). Luke doesn't actually depict Jesus being flogged.

- In Mark, it is quite clear that when Pilate ordered Jesus to be crucified, the Governor turned Jesus over to the Roman soldiers for that purpose (Mark 15:15–16). Luke and John both blur the issue and suggest that it was the Jews who crucified Jesus. In John, the relevant passage reads,

> They cried out, "Away with him! Away with him! Crucify him!" Pilate asked them, "Shall I crucify your King?" The chief priests answered, "We have no king but the emperor." Then he handed him over to them to be crucified. So they took Jesus; and carrying the cross by himself, he went out to what is called The Place of the Skull, which in Hebrew is called Golgotha. There they crucified him, and with him two others, one on either side, with Jesus between them. (John 19:15–18)

The phrasing clearly leaves the impression that Pilate turned Jesus over to the Jews for the purpose of crucifixion. Luke has a similar arrangement. At the key point of the narrative he has the following.

> But they kept urgently demanding with loud shouts that he should be crucified; and their voices prevailed. So Pilate gave his verdict that their demand should be granted. He released the man they asked for, the one who had been put in prison for insurrection and murder, and he handed Jesus over as they wished. As they led him away, they seized a man, Simon of Cyrene, who was coming from the country, and they laid the cross on him, and made him carry it behind Jesus. (Luke 23:23–26)

Here, too, the phrasing clearly implies that Pilate handed Jesus over to the Jews for crucifixion and that they carried out the sentence. Luke continues to foster that impression by the continued use of the vague "they" to identify the actors. Lest there be any doubt as to who Luke meant to suggest, later on after the resurrection, a traveler says to the resurrected but unrecognized Jesus, "our chief priests and leaders handed him over to be condemned to death *and crucified him*" (Luke 24:20, emphasis added). The referent for "they" would be the "chief priests and leaders."

From the examples above it is easy to see why some scholars vociferously argue that there must be some sort of a literary relationship between John and Luke, at least with regard to the Passion story.

The Raising of Lazarus

Another area that generates a good deal of debate about parallels between John and Luke revolves around the stories of Lazarus. Both John and Luke have a story about a character named Lazarus who died, but the stories are very different and quite inconsistent.

In John, Lazarus is a real person and Jesus raises him from the dead to live in his earthly form. It is made clear in the story that this raising from the dead is separate and apart from the more traditional view of the dead being lifted up to heaven in the afterlife. In Luke's story about someone named Lazarus, it is evident that the story is a parable and that Lazarus may not have been a real person. In Luke's account it is clear that the raising of Lazarus from the dead is associated with the rising up to heaven in the afterlife. Let's take a closer look at the two stories.

John's Lazarus

In all of John there is only one individual known as Lazarus and he figures in two closely related stories. First is the story of his being raised from the dead. The second is the incident of the anointing at Bethany, which took place in his home.

With regard to the anointing incident we have already noted some areas where Luke and John agree against Mark.

- In Luke and John, the anointing is to the feet; in Mark it is over the head.

- Both Luke and John had a chronological arrangement that placed the incident well before Mark did and both broke the connection between that story and the following story in Mark where Judas went to meet with the priests.
- Luke and John both moved the story to a different location than the one Mark had.
- Luke and John both had a slight change of tone from Mark. In Mark, the persons complaining about the expensive oil didn't appear to have any base motives. They were concerned with the poor. In Luke, the complainers are criticized for their lack of compassion and in John the complainer is Judas, who is motivated by greed.

According to John, Lazarus had two sisters, Martha and Mary (John 11:19). John said that Jesus had a close relationship with Lazarus and his two sisters (John 11:5). This is the only Martha who appears in John's Gospel.

The raising of Lazarus from the dead occurs a little before the anointing in Bethany. The story of Lazarus begins with the statement, "Now a certain man was ill, Lazarus of Bethany, the village of Mary and her sister Martha" (John 11:1). Oddly, as part of the introduction to the first story John says that this Mary was the one who anointed Jesus with perfume (John 11:2), which doesn't occur until the second story.

Jesus received a message from the sisters and said, "This illness does not lead to death; rather it is for God's glory, so that the Son of God may be glorified through it" (John 11:4). Jesus delayed his journey for a couple of days and eventually arrived after Lazarus has been entombed for four days (John 11:17). The sisters confronted Jesus about his delay leading to Lazarus's death and Jesus assures them that Lazarus will rise if they have faith (John 11:25).

Jesus eventually brings Lazarus back to life and this led to a great increase in Jesus' popularity. According to John the raising of Lazarus had made Jesus so popular that the High Priest feared that the Romans would destroy the Jewish polity and that Jesus must be put to death to save the nation (John 11:48). In John, the raising of Lazarus from the dead is the trigger event that leads the Jews to arrest Jesus and turn him over to Pilate. Despite the key role this event plays in John's Gospel, it goes completely unmentioned in the Synoptic Gospels. For Mark, the explanation for the arrest of Jesus is simply that the priests had become jealous of his popularity, but no mention is made of any Roman hostility (Mark 15:10).

Before turning to Luke's Lazarus story I should note that in the anointing in Bethany story, John depicts Martha as serving a meal and Mary at Jesus' feet anointing him (John 12:2–3).

Luke's Lazarus Story

Like John, Luke has only one character in his Gospel named Lazarus and only one character in his Gospel named Martha. Neither Mark nor Matthew has a Lazarus or a Martha in their Gospel. While John depicts Lazarus and Martha as brother and sister, Luke makes no connection between the two, but there is some reason, however, to think that Luke's Martha is the same person as John's Martha.

In the course of his mission, Jesus made a stop at an unidentified village, "where a woman named Martha welcomed him into her home. She had a sister named Mary, who sat at the Lord's feet and listened to what he was saying" (Luke 10:38–39). This led Martha to complain that she had to do all the work while Mary just sat around listening to Jesus. She asked him to tell Mary to help her out but Jesus declined (Luke 10:40).

Jesus responded, "Martha, Martha, you are worried and distracted by many things; there is need of only one thing. Mary has chosen the better part, which will not be taken away from her" (Luke 10:41–42).

Even though Luke does not depict this story as an anointing story or place it at Bethany, it is difficult not to see a close parallel between this episode and John's version of the anointing at Bethany incident. In both Gospels:

- There is only one woman named Martha;
- This Martha has a sister named Mary;
- This sister Mary sits at Jesus' feet;
- Martha is doing the household work;
- Someone complains about Mary's actions;
- Jesus' criticizes the complainer;
- Jesus praises Mary for her good work.

At the same time that we have these parallels, Luke also knows Mark's story about the anointing at Bethany and has significantly changed it around in a way that has him agree with John against Mark about certain details. This raises a host of questions.

Was the Martha/Mary story originally an independent literary unit unrelated to the anointing at Bethany? If so did John graft it on to the underlying anointing story in order to serve his own special editorial purposes? If not, did Luke modify the story to separate it from an anointing story? Did John invent a relationship between Lazarus and Martha or did Luke omit it? How one answers these questions will probably depend on one's theory about the existence of a literary relationship between John and Luke.

While the Martha/Mary story adds to the collection of parallels between John and Luke, it doesn't resolve the underlying issue of whether there is a connection between the Lazaruses in John and Luke. That said, let's look at Luke's Lazarus account.

Luke presents the story as a parable (Luke 16:19–31). According to Luke there were a rich man and a poor man. The poor man, named Lazarus, suffered from illnesses and sores. The rich man ignored the poor man and continued to live the luxurious life. Both men died. Lazarus was taken up to heaven where he dwelled with Abraham. The rich man awoke in Hades to great torment and saw Lazarus and Abraham off in a distance. The rich man begged Abraham to send Lazarus over to him with a little water to alleviate his thirst. Abraham responded that the rich man had received the good things during his earthly life while Lazarus only received evil things, and each now had the proper reward. Abraham added that a great chasm divided the two and no one can cross over. The rich man then begged Abraham to send Lazarus to the rich man's five brothers and warn them about what's to come. Abraham said that all that is necessary is that they listen to Moses and the prophets. The rich man replied that a visit from a resurrected man will lead them to repent. Abraham replied, "If they do not listen to Moses and the prophets, neither will they be convinced even if someone rises from the dead" Luke 16:31).

The Two Lazarus Stories Compared

Both Lazarus stories deal with the raising of Lazarus from the dead. In Luke the story is a parable and in John it is an actual event. A very key difference is that Luke's Lazarus does not appear before the living and John's Lazarus does. In John, Lazarus's appearance seems to be a fulfillment of the rich man's request that is denied in Luke. If John were using the parable as a source he would be acting to contradict the fundamental message that no appearance of the resurrected is necessary, as Moses and the prophets address the issue. On the other hand, John has a separate passage in which this theme arises.

Early in the mission, during the Sabbath violation story in John 5, Jesus debates with the Jews over whether he has done anything wrong. In a key passage there is a debate over the issue of eternal life. "You search the scriptures because you think that in them you have eternal life; and it is they that testify on my behalf. Yet you refuse to come to me to have life" (John 5:39–40). This is essentially the message of Luke's Lazarus parable. To emphasize the point, Jesus adds, "Do not think that I will accuse you before the Father; your accuser is Moses, on whom you have set your hope" (John 5:45).

We should also keep in mind that Luke also has stories about the raising of a dead man that doesn't appear in Mark or Matthew, although the man in this story is unnamed (Luke 7:11–17).[113] This raising of the dead man in Luke contributed significantly to Jesus' reputation (Luke 7:17).

In Luke, therefore, we find Jesus raised a man from the dead, a Martha/Mary story, and a parable about Lazarus being raised from the dead, and in the parable a direction to rely on the teachings of Moses to achieve eternal life. Did John read Luke and meld these various elements into his own Gospel story in which the dead man raised in Luke merged with the Lazarus in Luke's parable? Did he share a common source with Luke? Or do we simply have a coincidence with no connection between the stories? You can get good arguments on all of these viewpoints.

SUMMARY

John obviously knows a great many stories that also appear in one or more Synoptic Gospels but did he know any of the Synoptic Gospels when writing his own Gospel? This is a hotly contested issue among scholars and one that can't be easily resolved. In this chapter we looked at a number of illustrations that show why such a substantial debate exists. One key problem that frequently emerges is that John's language is often very different in form or style from that of the Synoptic Gospels. We noted, for example, that John appears to have taken a story about Jesus using a bread metaphor for teachings about eternal life and overlaid it with a highly spiritual literary teaching about the Eucharist that he transferred from the Last Supper.

We began with a look at the story of the anointing in Bethany and saw that John seems to incorporate factual elements that seem unique to either Mark, or Matthew or Luke. We saw that he agreed with Mark that the perfume was nard and that it cost 300 denarii, two facts not mentioned in Matthew and Luke. We also noticed that he agreed with Luke that the anointing was on the feet instead of over the head, as it appears in Mark and Matthew. And finally, we noticed that he makes the complainer in the story one of the disciples, a fact alluded to in Matthew but not in Mark or Luke.

From there we looked at a lengthy sequence in John 5–6 and saw a striking indication of sequential agreement between Mark and John for a large number of stories. A long sequence of story agreements suggests the existence of a written source, indicating that John copied from Mark or both knew a common written source. On the other hand there was often very little verbal agreement and many of the stories differed in content or style.

Finally, we looked at some evidence that John and Luke may have known a common Passion source that differed from Mark on many details. As with the Mark agreements, however, the verbal content and story elements occasionally varied by enough to raise questions as to whether a literary connection existed.

CHAPTER 4

Pilate's Dialogues in John

Evidence for a Lost Written Passion Narrative

*A*ll four Gospels authors organize their story of the Roman proceedings against Jesus around a basic template. The core story in all four Gospels consists of the following incidents. Jews accuse Jesus of many crimes; Pilate conducts an inquiry into charges that Jesus claimed to be King of the Jews; Pilate offers to release Jesus but the Jews reject that offer, demanding instead that Pilate release an anti-Roman rebel named Barabbas; the Jews demand that Jesus be crucified and Pilate argues with them; Pilate hands Jesus over for crucifixion; Jesus is flogged; Roman soldiers (Herodian soldiers in Luke) mock Jesus as King of the Jews; and Jesus is led out to be crucified. Despite agreement on the skeletal structure, the four Gospels differ radically with regard to many details within the scenes and as to the sequence of events.

One important difference between John and the Synoptic Gospels is that John's version of this event contains a longer dialogue between Pilate and Jesus and a longer dialogue between Pilate and the Jews than the Synoptic Gospels do. In Mark the two dialogues with Pilate appear in a simple straight-line narrative. Pilate makes inquiry of Jesus and then engages in a dialogue with the Jews. All the action takes place in the one location. John, in addition to longer dialogues, breaks each dialogue into separate segments. The interview with Jesus has two separate portions and the confrontation with the Jews has four different sections. John uses changes of location or the insertion of other events, such as the mocking of Jesus by the Roman soldiers, to separate the various dialogue segments.

Luke, although he uses Mark as a source, seems to agree with John on several details of the appearance before Pilate that don't appear in Mark.

- In John and Luke, Pilate declares Jesus innocent on three separate occasions; in Mark and Matthew, Pilate never declares Jesus innocent of the charges.
- In John, the crowd cries out "Crucify him! Crucify him!" and in Luke, "Crucify, crucify him!"; in Mark and Matthew the crowd only shouts out "Crucify him!", using the word "crucify" only once where John and Luke have it used twice in the same demand.
- In John and Luke, Pilate expresses an interest in where Jesus comes from; Mark and Matthew have no such concern.
- In John and Luke, Pilate calls for the flogging of Jesus before he orders the crucifixion; in Mark and Matthew, the flogging occurs after the verdict.
- In John and Luke, the proceedings shift around to different locations; in Mark and Matthew everything happens in one location.
- In John and Luke, ambiguous narrative makes it appear that Pilate handed Jesus over to the Jews for crucifixion; in Mark and Matthew, it is clear that Pilate handed Jesus over to the Roman soldiers for crucifixion.

These sorts of parallels between John and Luke, as we noted in the previous chapter, have led many New Testament historians to believe that there was some sort of literary relationship between Luke and John, but the precise nature of that relationship is subject to substantial debate.

In this chapter I want to put forth an argument that there existed a written Passion Narrative that influenced both John and Luke. At the conclusion of the argument I will raise some questions as to whether Mark also knew this Passion Narrative and modified it so that it varied from what John and Luke set down or whether this written narrative supplanted Mark's account or the source that Mark relied on.

At the heart of my argument is the existence of several anomalies in John's account of the dialogues between Pilate and Jesus and Pilate and the Jews. It strikes me that not only do some of the questions and answers in these dialogues seem to be out of chronological order, but it also seems that some of the answers belong to different questions. In the course of my analysis I will attempt to reconstruct what seems to be the more likely logical order of the dialogues, one which eliminates the anomalies and provides for a smoother literary flow. If my proposed reconstruction holds up to scrutiny it would indicate that John must have used a written source for his account and made radical changes to it.

Pilate's Interrogation of Jesus

Table 4.1 sets out in narrative order the complete dialogue in John between Pilate and Jesus. I have stripped it of all the surrounding text and narrative breaks, showing only the actual dialogue as it unfolds. Column 1 divides the dialogue into textual units and gives a number to each one to reflect the actual sequential order in John. I have also divided both the third and sixth textual units into subunits, 3a, 3b, 6a and 6b. Column 2 contains the verse citations. Column 3 indicates who the speaker is. Column 4 contains the dialogue passages. Speech by Jesus is set forth in bold type. Note that there is a break in the dialogue between items 7 and 8, as a number of other matters take place in the intervening period.

In this section I want to first look at how Mark's version of the Pilate-Jesus dialogue surfaces in John and then I will suggest that there seems to be something odd about the arrangement of some of the questions and answers. In the next section I will propose a reconstruction of the Pilate-Jesus dialogue that seems to make much more logical sense as a narrative flow of events.

Pilate's Questions

In Mark, Pilate asks only two questions of Jesus and receives only two responses, one verbal, and one silent.

Pilate asked him, "Are you the King of the Jews?" He answered him, "You say so." Then the chief priests accused him of many things. Pilate

TABLE 4.1 Dialogue Between Pilate and Jesus in the Gospel of John

The sequence of statements in Column 4 appears in the same order that it does in the Gospel of John. Column 1 assigns a sequence number to each statement. For later convenience statements 3 and 6 are divided into two parts. Statements by Jesus are in bold face.

Order	Verse	Speaker	Statement
1	18:33	Pilate	Are you the king of the Jews?
2	18:34	Jesus	**Do you ask this on your own, or did others tell you about me?**
3a	18:35	Pilate	I am not a Jew, am I?
3b	18:35	Pilate	Your own nation and the chief priests have handed you over to me. What have you done?
4	18:36	Jesus	**My kingdom is not from this world. If my kingdom were from this world, my followers would be fighting to keep me from being handed over to the Jews. But as it is, my kingdom is not from here.**
5	18:37	Pilate	So you are a king?
6a	18:37	Jesus	**You say that I am a king.**
6b	18:37	Jesus	**For this I was born, and for this I came into the world, to testify to the truth. Everyone who belongs to the truth listens to my voice.**
7	18:38	Pilate	What is truth?
			Break in dialogue: Pilate speaks to the crowd.
8	19:9	Pilate	Where are you from?
9	19:9	Jesus	**But Jesus gave him no answer.**
10	19:10	Pilate	Do you refuse to speak to me? Do you not know that I have power to release you, and power to crucify you?
11	19:11	Jesus	**You would have no power over me unless it had been given you from above; therefore the one who handed me over to you is guilty of a greater sin.**

asked him again, "Have you no answer? See how many charges they bring against you." But Jesus made no further reply, so that Pilate was amazed. (Mark 15:2–5)

This is the full interrogation of Jesus by Pilate according to Mark. His narrative raises some questions. First, when Jesus says to Pilate "You say so," he is wrong. Pilate didn't say so. He simply asked if that was the case. This hints at the idea that Jesus' response must have originally been to a stronger accusation than the one portrayed here. Second, it's hard to imagine how this questioning and the responses by Jesus could in any way convince Pilate that Jesus should be released. In John's dialogue, both of these issues appear to be addressed.

Now let's look at the first two questions by Pilate in John and Jesus' responses. The parallels to Mark are in bold face. In Table 4.1 the specific dialogue appears as textual units 1–4.

Then Pilate entered the headquarters again, summoned Jesus, and asked him, "**Are you the King of the Jews?**" Jesus answered, "Do you ask this on your own, or did others tell you about me?" Pilate replied, "I am not a Jew, am I? Your own nation and the chief priests have handed you over to me. **What have you done?**" Jesus answered, "My kingdom is not from this world. If my kingdom were from this world, my followers would be fighting to keep me from being handed over to the Jews. But as it is, my kingdom is not from here." (John 18:33–36)

In John, Pilate's first two questions (more specifically textual units 1 and 3b) correspond, in substance, directly to Pilate's first two questions in Mark. In both Gospels Pilate asks Jesus if he is the King of the Jews and then asks Jesus to respond to the charges against him. But as you can see, the responses from John's Jesus are radically different from the responses by Mark's Jesus.

As to the first question, where Mark has Jesus respond with "You say so," John's Jesus responds by asking where Pilate got his information from. As to the second question, eliciting a response to the charges being brought against him, where Mark has silence John's Jesus sets forth a theological description of the nature of his kingdom, saying it is not of this earth. So Mark and John begin with the same two basic questions from Pilate, but John's Jesus gives two very different responses than Mark's Jesus. Curiously, however, the two missing answers from Mark's Jesus also appear in John, but as responses to different questions.

Jesus' Responses

Following Jesus' response to the second question from Pilate, John continues with the following passage. The parallel to Mark is in bold. This part of the dialogue appears in Table 4.1 as textual units 5–6b.

> Pilate asked him, "So you are a king?" Jesus answered, "**You say that I am a king**. For this I was born, and for this I came into the world, to testify to the truth. Everyone who belongs to the truth listens to my voice." (John 18:37)

In this narrative section Pilate responds to Jesus' theological claim about a non-earthly kingdom with a direct accusation, "So you are a king?" It is to this direct accusation that Jesus responds with a variation of Mark's "You say so." As I noted above, in Mark, Jesus' response seemed out of order in that Pilate hadn't made an accusation but only asked a question. I suggested that this hinted at the possibility of a more forceful accusation in an earlier version of the story. Here, John addresses that problem by having Pilate make an accusation based on a theological misunderstanding of what Jesus professes to be and Jesus' answer implies that Pilate misunderstood what Jesus had just explained to him.

A possible problem with John's arrangement is that the explanation that triggered the misunderstanding was not responsive to the question that Pilate asked. Pilate had asked Jesus to respond to the charges against him and Jesus avoided that response by giving a theological statement about the nature of his kingdom. On the other hand, it is not hard to see how John might have thought that this was an appropriate response, given John's theological perspective.

The second part of Jesus' answer, about being born to the truth also presents a problem. It doesn't seem to address Pilate's lack of comprehension. The issue immediately before Pilate is not credibility but clarity of expression. Pilate has essentially said, "So what is it? Are you or aren't you a king." Jesus' claim to being born to the truth doesn't seem to clarify matters.

That Jesus' explanation seems somewhat muddled in this context is apparent from Pilate's response, "What is truth?" (John 18:38). Although many scholars treat this statement as if it reflects a deep philosophical contemplation on Pilate's part, the context suggests otherwise. Pilate's question is rhetorical and he doesn't even bother to explore the "truth" further with Jesus. Instead, Pilate gets up and leaves. His reaction suggests more a frustrated lack of comprehension than deep thought.

When Pilate returns back outside he announces to the crowd that he finds no case against Jesus. However, that is not what he said just a few moments earlier, when he accused Jesus of being a king. Basically, John's Pilate seems to display no understanding of what Jesus is talking about and as his later actions demonstrate he treats Jesus' claim to kingship as more a matter for ridicule than as a serious threat. It is this understanding that later leads Pilate and the Roman guards to mock and abuse Jesus as King of the Jews and to argue that the Jews should let him go.

During the break in the interrogation of Jesus Pilate has a confrontation with the Jews and one of the allegations from the crowd appears to leave him somewhat shaken (John 19:8). Pilate immediately "entered his headquarters again and asked Jesus, 'Where are you from?' But **Jesus gave him no answer**" (John 19:9, emphasis added).

This response from Jesus corresponds to Mark's second response from Jesus, silence, but Jesus gives this to an entirely different question and his response seems out of character. In the first place, a fundamental theme in John is that Jesus was sent from Heaven, and Jesus preaches that doctrine frequently in the Gospel. Pilate's question about where Jesus comes from seems to be the natural lead-in for some remark by Jesus about his heavenly origin. Second, what makes this silence even stranger is that Jesus has already told Pilate that his kingdom is not from this world. Having said that, why would Jesus suddenly clam up when it comes to addressing a fundamental doctrine of his ministry? This sequence of Jesus' silence about where he comes from after talking about his kingdom not being from this world suggests a chronological problem with the order of John's narrative.

If we switched Jesus' second answer (textual unit 4 in Table 4.1) with Jesus' fourth answer (textual unit 9 in Table 4.1) the logical flow would seem a better fit. It would have John and Mark both agree that when Pilate asked Jesus to address the charges he remained silent, and the speech about his kingdom not being from this world would fit in better with the question about where Jesus came from.

In any event, in response to Jesus' silence, according to John, Pilate challenged him further. "Do you refuse to speak to me? Do you not know that I have power to release you, and power to crucify you?" (John 19:10). Pilate's follow-up suggests a further chronological problem. At this point in time Pilate has made three public declarations that he found no case against Jesus. Why would Jesus' silence as to the question of where he came from provoke a threat of crucifixion? In terms of narrative flow, one suspects that this question must have originally come earlier in the sequence of events.

Summary of the Problem with Pilate's Interrogation of Jesus

In this section we saw that John and Mark both depict Pilate asking Jesus the same two first questions but that the two Gospels disagreed as to what answers were given. We also saw that parallels to Mark's two answers by Jesus appeared in John with regard to Pilate's third and fifth questions (assuming that the unanswered question—What is truth?—was the fourth question). In reviewing the material I suggested that the second and fourth answers in John appear to be inconsistent with narrative logic and would make more sense if they were reversed. Such a reversal would bring John into line with Mark as to Jesus' silence when asked to respond to the charges and make a better fit to Pilate's question about where Jesus came from. We also noted that Pilate's threat to execute Jesus in the wake of his silence seemed to be inconsistent with the Governor's three prior declarations of innocence.

A Proposed Reconstruction of John's Dialogue between Pilate and Jesus

Table 4.2 sets forth my proposed reconstruction of what I believe to be the original narrative order underlying John's dialogue between Pilate and Jesus. I have rearranged the textual units in a manner that I believe addresses the problems discussed above and which provides a more logical and smoother narrative flow than John presently has. To the extent that this stands up to scrutiny, it would suggest that there must have been an underlying written source that was re-arranged. In considering this solution reserve final judgment until I complete the analysis of Pilate's dialogue with the Jews, which I believe will strengthen the conclusion suggested here.

In the following reconstruction the numbers in parenthesis in front of the text are the textual unit numbers given in Table 4.1. I start with Mark's first question and answer and replicate it in John. In the proposed reconstruction John's textual source would now begin with the following question and answer.

> (1) "Are you the King of the Jews?"
> (6a) "You say that I am a king."

This initially brings John into line with Mark who starts the same way. As I noted above, however, Jesus' reply in Mark seemed inappropriate to Pilate's question, as Pilate had not said that Jesus was the king of the Jews but only asked if that was so. In this reconstruction Pilate picks up on that discrepancy and responds to the accusation from Jesus, indicating that the charges came from the Jews, not from him.

> (3a) "I am not a Jew, am I?"

Faced with an apparent accusation from the Jewish authorities, Jesus attempts to rebut the accusation by describing himself as a prophet-type figure here to preach the truth to those who will listen. But he doesn't specifically deny being the King of the Jews.

TABLE 4.2 Proposed Reconstruction of the Source Used by the Author
of the Gospel of John for the Dialogue Between Pilate and Jesus

This table shows the proposed reconstruction of the source used by the author of the Gospel of John. The numbers in Column 1 are the statement numbers assigned to each statement in Table 4.1. The statement numbers enable you to see how the author of the Gospel of John rearranged the questions and answers. Statements by Jesus are in bold face. Items in brackets may be Johannine additions to the original source.

Order	Verse	Speaker	Statement
1	18:33	Pilate	Are you the king of the Jews?
6a	18:37	Jesus	**You say that I am a king.**
3a	18:35	Pilate	I am not a Jew, am I?
6b	18:37	Jesus	**For this I was born, and for this I came into the world, to testify to the truth. Everyone who belongs to the truth listens to my voice.**
7	18:38	Pilate	What is truth?
2	18:34	Jesus	**Do you ask this on your own, or did others tell you about me?**
3b	18:35	Pilate	Your own nation and the chief priests have handed you over to me. What have you done?
9	19:9	Jesus	**But Jesus gave him no answer.**
10	19:10	Pilate	Do you refuse to speak to me? Do you not know that I have power to release you, and power to crucify you?
11	19:11	Jesus	**You would have no power over me unless it had been given you from above; [therefore the one who handed me over to you is guilty of a greater sin.]**
8	19:9	Pilate	Where are you from?
4	18:36	Jesus	**My kingdom is not from this world. [If my kingdom were from this world, my followers would be fighting to keep me from being handed over to the Jews. But as it is, my kingdom is not from here.]**
5	18:37	Pilate	So you are a king?

(6b) "For this I was born, and for this I came into the world, to testify
to the truth. Everyone who belongs to the truth listens to my voice."

Pilate, however, presses further. He is still not quite sure what it is
that Jesus claims to be and asks what truth Jesus is teaching vis-à-vis his
role as a king.

(7) "What is truth?"

Pilate's question about "truth" leaves Jesus wondering if Pilate is simply curious about what Jesus has explained and wants further discussion
or is an indication that he wants a response to the Jewish charges. So he
inquires of Pilate why he is asking the question.

(2) "Do you ask this on your own, or did others tell you about me?"

Pilate, apparently annoyed at the evasions, reminds Jesus that he has
been turned over by the Jewish authorities, and wants to know what he
did wrong. This brings us to Mark's second question and Jesus falls silent
rather than acknowledge any wrong doing, just as Mark has it.

(3b) "Your own nation and the chief priests have handed you over to
me. What have you done?"
(9) "But Jesus gave no answer"

Pilate, as would be expected, did not consider silence an option. He reminds Jesus of the consequences of not answering. But Jesus shows no fear.

(10) Pilate therefore said to him, "Do you refuse to speak to me? Do
you not know that I have power to release you, and power to
crucify you?"
(11) Jesus answered him, "You would have no power over me unless
it had been given you from above; therefore the one who handed
me over to you is guilty of a greater sin."

The reference to power coming from heaven leads Pilate to ask Jesus where he comes from. Jesus responds with the statement that his kingdom is not from this world.

(8) "Where are you from?"

(4) "My kingdom is not from this world. If my kingdom were from this world, my followers would be fighting to keep me from being handed over to the Jews. But as it is, my kingdom is not from here."

With Jesus talking about having a kingdom, the theological nature of which Pilate fails to grasp, the Roman Governor concludes indeed that Jesus does claim to be a king.

(5) "So you are a king."

This brings us to the end of the dialogue with Jesus, Pilate concluding that Jesus claims to be some sort of king but, with all this talk about heaven, Pilate concludes that Jesus' claim to being a king is somewhat nonsensical and not a threat to the government. In this reconstructed source Pilate would have followed up this determination with a flogging and an offer to release Jesus. But no doubt, if this reconstruction is correct, the source went on to depict the Jews in opposition to any release.

In the reconstructed form we saw the broad original outline in Mark. The first part of the reconstruction involves jockeying around the accusation that Jesus is the king of the Jews and Jesus' efforts to avoid giving a direct answer to that question. This is followed by Pilate asking Jesus to comment on the charges against him and Jesus refusing to answer to accusations from the Jewish authorities.

Appended to this, however, is Pilate's determination that Jesus did claim to be some sort of king but that the claim, enmeshed in this talk about heaven, indicated that Jesus was more a figure of ridicule than any serious threat. This attitude is actually reflected in John by his portrayal of Pilate and the soldiers mocking Jesus as King of the Jews, ridiculing

Jesus by placing him in royal robes and a crown of thorns, whipping him, and showing Jesus off to the crowd as a bloodied ridiculous clown-king (John 19:1–6).

In the next section I look at Pilate's dialogue with the Jews and we will see further evidence that John has been re-arranging an earlier written source.

PILATE'S DIALOGUE WITH THE JEWS

John breaks up the dialogue between Pilate and the Jews into four separate segments. In Table 4.3 I have set forth the entire dialogue following John's narrative order and indicated where the breaks are. The table is organized in the same manner as Table 4.1, with the numbers in Column 1 representing the sequence of textual units. I have divided the fifth textual unit into two parts, 5a and 5b.

An important defect in Mark's Gospel, at least from a narrative point of view, is that he doesn't tell us why Jesus has been brought to Pilate for punishment. Why didn't the Jews try Jesus themselves and implement their own punishment? Why did they have to go to Pilate to have Jesus punished? We are told that the "the chief priests accused him of many things" (Mark 15:3) but we are not told what charges they brought to Pilate. Eventually, of course, Pilate has Jesus executed for violating Roman law by claiming to be King of the Jews (Mark 15:26). But that charge is not specifically set forth in the complaint to Pilate. John's Gospel rectifies that problem.

In John, Pilate begins by asking the Jews, "What accusation do you bring against this man?" (John 18:29). As in Mark the accusations by the Jews are not specified. "If this man were not a criminal, we would not have handed him over to you" (John 18:30). This is sort of like saying, "Beats me. You figure out what he did wrong." Pilate, apparently annoyed at the lack of specificity, tells the Jews to take Jesus and try him themselves according to their own law (John 18:31). Pilate seems to be saying, "if you won't tell me what he did, don't bother me with your

TABLE 4.3 Dialogue Between Pilate and the Jews from The Gospel of John

The sequence of statements in Column 4 appears in the same order as it does in the Gospel of John. Column 1 assigns a sequential statement number to each section of dialogue. For later convenience, Statement #5 is divided into two parts, 5a and 5b. Statements attributed to the Jews are in bold face.

Order	Verse	Speaker	Statement
1	18:29	Pilate	What accusation do you bring against this man?
2	18:30	Jews	**If this man were not a criminal, we would not have handed him over to you.**
3	18:31	Pilate	Take him yourselves and judge him according to your law.
4	18:31	Jews	**We are not permitted to put anyone to death.**
			Break in dialogue: Pilate goes inside to question Jesus
5a	18:38	Pilate	I find no case against him.
5b	18:39	Pilate	But you have a custom that I release someone for you at the Passover. Do you want me to release for you the King of the Jews?
6	18:40	Jews	**Not this man, but Barabbas!**
			Mockery and abuse of Jesus
7	19:4-5	Pilate	Look, I am bringing him out to you to let you know that I find no case against him. (So Jesus came out, wearing the crown of thorns and the purple robe.) Here is the man!
8	19:6	Jews	**Crucify him! Crucify him!**
9	19:6	Pilate	Take him yourselves and crucify him; I find no case against him.
10	19:7	Jews	**We have a law, and according to that law he ought to die because he has claimed to be the Son of God.**
			Break in dialogue. Pilate returns to question Jesus further
11	19:12	Pilate	(From then on Pilate tried to release him.)

Order	Verse	Speaker	Statement
12	19:12	Jews	If you release this man, you are no friend of the emperor. Everyone who claims to be a king sets himself against the emperor.
13	19:14	Pilate	Here is your King!
14	19:15	Jews	Away with him! Away with him! Crucify him!
15	19:15	Pilate	Shall I crucify your King?
16	19:15	Jews	We have no king but the emperor.

problems." We should recall here that in John, unlike Mark, there was no Jewish trial of Jesus prior to going to Pilate and no charges had been voted against him.

The Jews respond to Pilate, "We are not permitted to put anyone to death" (John 18:31). This explains why Jews need to turn Jesus over to Pilate. He has to implement the death penalty. Reluctantly, he agrees to hear the case.[114] Jesus had previously been placed inside Pilate's headquarters while the Jews remained outside (for purity reasons). Pilate leaves the Jewish authorities and goes into his headquarters to begin his interrogation of Jesus.

This initial dialogue between Pilate and the Jews seems somewhat inconsistent and out of chronological order with a later portion of the dialogue. After the Barabbas incident and after the mockery, abuse and flogging of Jesus, Pilate brings Jesus out before the crowd in bloodied mock royal finery and says "here is the man" (John 19:4–5).

The Jews react by crying out, "Crucify him! Crucify him (John 19:6)!"

Pilate responds, "Take him yourselves and crucify him; I find no case against him" (John 19:6).

Here we encounter a couple of problems. First, Pilate has already been told by the Jews that they can't put anyone to death. So why would he tell the Jews to take Jesus and crucify him? Second, instead of reminding Pilate that they can't put anyone to death, as we should expect, they introduce for the first time a claim by the Jews that they "have a law, and according to that law he ought to die because he has claimed to be the Son of God" (John 19:7). Shouldn't this have been mentioned earlier, when Pilate asked them what the charges were? There seems to be some chronological inconsistencies in the flow of the dialogue. More logically, we would expect Pilate to ask what the charges were; the Jews would tell him about the law requiring death; Pilate would tell the Jews to try Jesus themselves; and the Jews would respond that they can't put anyone to death. But that is not what we have here.

Here's another chronological inconsistency. After Pilate's initial examination of Jesus, he came back out of his headquarters and told the Jewish crowd, "I find no case against him" (John 19:38). At this point Pilate pointed out that there was a custom of having the Governor release a prisoner over the Passover holidays and asks if he should release "the King of the Jews" (John 18:38–39). The Jews rejected the offer and asked for the release of Barabbas (John 18:40). (In John, Pilate never releases Barabbas, but instead has Jesus flogged and the Roman soldiers mock and abuse him.) Later, after further questioning of Jesus, John tells us "From then on Pilate tried to release him" but the Jews opposed his action (John 19:123).

This allegation about Pilate trying to release Jesus "from then on" seems out of chronological order. He had already been trying to release Jesus earlier, right after the first interview with Jesus when he declared that he found no case against him. Let's review that scene again for further difficulties.

When Pilate came out after the first interview with Jesus and said he found no case against him, he immediately raised the question of releasing a prisoner over the holidays. Let's put aside here the problem that in Mark it is Jews in the crowd who raise the issue of a prisoner release and not Pilate. In terms of John's narrative flow this sequence doesn't make sense. Pilate had just declared that he found Jesus innocent. It was his initial duty therefore to release him. He should not have to raise the holiday release issue unless some opposition had been voiced to the release. But no opposition had yet been raised. Why didn't he simply announce,

"Therefore I am releasing him"? If opposition arose, then he would consider raising the holiday appeal.

This suggests that the later reference to Pilate, from then on wanting to release Jesus, actually belongs earlier in the story, after the first declaration that Pilate found no case against Jesus, and that the holiday offer followed at some point after that reference.

A PROPOSED RECONSTRUCTION OF JOHN'S DIALOGUE BETWEEN PILATE AND THE JEWS

Table 4.4 sets forth my proposed reconstruction of Pilate's dialogue between Jesus and the Jews. I have rearranged the textual units in a manner that I believe addresses the chronological problems discussed above and which provides a more logical and smoother narrative flow than John presently has. Again, to the extent that this reconstruction stands up to scrutiny, together with the earlier reconstruction of the dialogue between Jesus and Pilate, this evidence would strongly suggest that John had a written source and rearranged the text. The numbers in parenthesis represent the textual unit numbers from Table 4.3.

I begin again with an opening that parallels Mark, the filing by Jewish authorities of unspecified charges against Jesus.

(1) So Pilate went out to them and said, "What accusation do you bring against this man?" (John 18:29)

(2) They answered, "If this man were not a criminal, we would not have handed him over to you." (John 18:30)

At this point there would have been an interrogation of Jesus by Pilate, after which Pilate would announce that he finds Jesus innocent of wrongdoing and prepares to release him. Pilate's concern here would only have been with violation of Roman law, not Jewish law.

(5a) "I find no case against him." (John 18:38)

(11) From then on Pilate tried to release him. (John 19:12)

TABLE 4.4 Proposed Reconstruction of the Source Used by the Author of John for the Dialogue Between Pilate and the Jews

The numbers in Column 1 are the statement numbers assigned to each statement in Table 4.3. The statement numbers enable you to see how the author of the Gospel of John rearranged the statements. Statements attributed to the Jews are in bold face.

Order	Verse	Speaker	Statement
1	18:29	Pilate	What accusation do you bring against this man?
2	18:30	Jews	**If this man were not a criminal, we would not have handed him over to you.**
Break in dialogue: Pilate goes inside to question Jesus. Comes back out.			
5a	18:38	Pilate	I find no case against him.
11	19:12	Pilate	(From then on Pilate tried to release him.)
12	19:12	Jews	**If you release this man, you are no friend of the emperor. Everyone who claims to be a king sets himself against the emperor.**
5b	18:39	Pilate	But you have a custom that I release someone for you at the Passover. Do you want me to release for you the King of the Jews?
6	18:40	Jews	**Not this man, but Barabbas!**
15	19:15	Pilate	Shall I crucify your King?
14	19:15	Jews	**Away with him! Away with him! Crucify him!**
3	18:31	Pilate	Take him yourselves and judge him according to your law.
10	19:7	Jews	**We have a law, and according to that law he ought to die because he has claimed to be the Son of God.**
9	19:6	Pilate	Take him yourselves and crucify him; I find no case against him.
4	18:31	Jews	**We are not permitted to put anyone to death.**
Mockery and abuse of Jesus.			
13	19:14	Pilate	Here is your King!
16	19:15	Jews	**We have no king but the emperor.**

Order	Verse	Speaker	Statement
Pilate returns to question Jesus further.				

Order	Verse	Speaker	Statement
			Pilate returns to question Jesus further.
7	19:4-5	Pilate	Look, I am bringing him out to you to let you know that I find no case against him. (So Jesus came out, wearing the crown of thorns and the purple robe.) Here is the man!
8	19:6	Jews	**Crucify him! Crucify him!**

As I suggested above, Pilate's initial instincts after finding Jesus innocent of wrongdoing would be to release Jesus and only invoke the holiday amnesty after experiencing opposition to any release. That is the scenario I follow next. The Jews express opposition to the release and Pilate invokes the holiday tradition of release.

(12) "If you release this man, you are no friend of the emperor. Everyone who claims to be a king sets himself against the emperor." (John 19:12)

(5b) "But you have a custom that I release someone for you at the Passover. Do you want me to release for you the King of the Jews?" (John 18:39)

The Jews reject the offer of releasing Jesus and instead request the release of Barabbas.

(6) "Not this man, but Barabbas." (John 18:40)

This leads Pilate to ask if they are really requesting the crucifixion of Jesus, whom he refers to as "your king." As the reference to "your king" would have been offensive to the Jewish officials who rejected such a title, it should probably be taken as a sarcastic remark intended to reflect Pilate's belief that Jesus is a ridiculous figure and not deserving of execution.[115] The Jews respond with a demand that Jesus be crucified.

(15) "Shall I crucify your King?" (John 19:15)

(14) "Away with him! Away with him! Crucify him!" (John 19:15)

As we are given that Pilate wants to release Jesus because he finds him innocent and John portrays Pilate as somewhat contemptuous towards Jesus, Pilate acts to disengage himself from the proceedings. He treats the matter as merely a religious dispute between Jesus and the Jewish authorities. This contrasts with Mark 15:10, which says that Pilate knew that the Jewish authorities were acting out of jealousy towards Jesus. Pilate tells the Jews to deal with Jesus on their own terms. This demand triggers a discussion over the inability of the Jews to try the case.

> (3) "Take him yourselves and judge him according to your law."
> (John 18:31)
> (10) "We have a law, and according to that law he ought to die
> because he has claimed to be the Son of God." (John 19:7)
> (9) "Take him yourselves and crucify him; I find no case against
> him." (John 19:6)
> (4) "We are not permitted to put anyone to death." (John 18:31)

The above set of verses in this revised order solves the chronological disparities discussed earlier. As structured, Pilate now has to decide how to proceed next. I suggest that at this point in the underlying source Pilate had Jesus flogged and the Roman soldiers mocked and abused Jesus, presumably to offer some sort of punishment to satisfy the priests. In Luke, which appears to have drawn on sources similar to John's, he has Pilate declare, "I have found in him no ground for the sentence of death; I will therefore have him flogged and then release him" (Luke 23:22).

There is some ambiguity in John about how and when Jesus was brought before the crowd. At John 19:5 Jesus is brought out in his bloodied clown-king costume. At John 19:9 Pilate goes back into his headquarters to question Jesus further. There is no explicit claim that Jesus went back with him but it could be implied. At John 9:13 he is brought out again and there is further discussion with the Jewish authorities. In this reconstruction I will follow that sequence. Pilate brings Jesus out in his clown-king costume and offers him up as a figure of ridicule. Again he sarcastically refers to Jesus as "your king." But the Jews continue to oppose Pilate's efforts to release Jesus.

(13) "Here is your king!" (John 19:14)
(16) "We have no king but the emperor." (John 19:15)

At this point Pilate may have gone back inside with Jesus, had further discussions, and then returned back out with Jesus in tow. When the conversation with the Jews resumes there is an important shift in emphasis. Pilate no longer refers sarcastically to Jesus as "your King"; he refers to Jesus simply as a "man," underscoring that he finds no basis for putting him to death for claiming to be King of the Jews. Once again, the Jews reject his offer, and the dialogue comes to an end.

(7) "Look, I am bringing him out to you to let you know that I find no case against him." So Jesus came out, wearing the crown of thorns and the purple robe. Pilate said to them, "Here is the man!" (John 19:4–5)
(8) "Crucify him! Crucify him!" (John 19:6)

SUMMARY OF THE RECONSTRUCTED DIALOGUE WITH JESUS

The following outline summarizes the reordered narrative. I suggest that it not only solves the chronological anomalies in John's version but that it provides a simple chronological flow by episodes and generates a smoother narrative flow.

Outline of Reconstructed Dialogue

a. Pilate inquires into the charges and finds nothing wrong in terms of Roman law;
   i. He offers to release Jesus;
   ii. The Jews reject the offer;
   iii. Pilate brings up the holiday amnesty;
   iv. The Jews reject the offer;
b. Because he finds no violation of Roman law, Pilate tells the Jews to try Jesus themselves;

     i. They claim Jesus violated Jewish law and should be put to death;

     ii. Pilate tells the Jews to crucify Jesus themselves;

     iii. The Jews claim they can't put anyone to death;

  c. Pilate punishes Jesus by flogging and treats him as a figure of ridicule in the hope of satisfying the Jews;

     i. The Jews reject the offer;

     ii. Pilate says that Jesus is just a man, not a king;

     iii. The Jews demand crucifixion.

Why Did John Change the Order of Events?

Assuming the validity of the reconstructions above we should explore the question of why John would change the order of events in the two dialogues. When considering why Gospel authors altered the content in their textual sources its usually helpful to compare how the text unfolds in the source and how that text fits in with the Gospel author's theological framework. Doing so here can help resolve the problem. There are several portions of the reconstructed dialogue that seem to conflict with John's point of view.

In the proposed reconstruction of John's dialogue between Pilate and Jesus the pre-John structure took the following form: examination of the charge that Jesus claimed to be King of the Jews; examination of the charges brought against him by the Jewish leaders; and a verdict. In the reconstruction, Pilate ends with the conclusion that Jesus does claim to be a king of some sort. In context, however, Pilate finds that Jesus' claim to being a king is somewhat ridiculous and not much of a threat. He treats Jesus with contempt and the soldiers mock and abuse him.

In the first phase of the interrogation the reconstruction has Pilate catching Jesus out in a rhetorical error. Pilate had asked Jesus if he were the king of the Jews and Jesus responded, "You say I am a king." Pilate hadn't said that Jesus was a king; he had only asked a question. So Pilate responded, "I am not a Jew, am I?" The response indicates that Pilate believes that it is the Jews who are making the accusation and that Pilate, not being a Jew, is not making the accusation.

In John's theology Jesus is the perfect human, incapable of mistake, and always in control. Leaving the dialogue in the original form would show Jesus as less than perfect. So John needed to make some change to the order of the narrative to eliminate any implication of a mistake by Jesus.

A second major problem for John concerns the final verse of the reconstructed dialogue, where Pilate says, "So you are a king?" The Gospel authors, John included, did not want to portray Jesus as admitting to Pilate that he was a king. This would somehow justify Pilate's actions in having Jesus executed. The goal in all of the Gospels was to shift the blame from Pilate directly on to the Jews. Pilate was portrayed as acting because the Jews refused to acknowledge Jesus' true role. Leaving a verdict of "you are a king" as the final outcome of Pilate's interrogation undermined the emerging Christian theme of Jewish responsibility for the death of Jesus. John needed to rearrange the text so that wouldn't be the final resolution.

A similar theological problem emerged in John's presentation of the dialogue with the Jews. In the underlying reconstructed text, the final stage shows Jesus as a defeated humiliated figure and Pilate displays him before the Jews as "the man" rather than as "your king." When the Jews reject the offer to release Jesus in this final stage Pilate allows the crucifixion to take place.

Ending the scene with Pilate and the Jews treating Jesus as just "the man" probably seemed offensive and John appears to have moved the passage earlier and chosen to end the dialogue with the Jews rejecting any claim that Jesus can be a king. John's final verse in the Pilate-Jewish dialogue is "We have no king but the emperor" (John 19:15). This sets John's theological stage. Jews have totally rejected the heaven-sent Jesus for an earthly foreign king. The very next verse in John uses ambiguity to make it appear that the Jews themselves crucified Jesus. "Then he handed him over to them to be crucified" (John 19:16). This, despite John's earlier report that the Jews brought Jesus to Pilate because they couldn't put anyone to death.

Unfortunately, when you begin to move multiple pieces of a coherent narrative into different locations within the narrative you open up a host of problems, including continuity and chronology. John chose to overlook those defects in order to eliminate the negative theological implications of the underlying text. He wanted the narrative to clearly blame the Jews for Jesus' death in that they refused to accept Jesus as the son of the Father. Consequently, he accepted the inconsistencies and chronological problems he generated in order to set forth his larger theological theme of Jewish guilt.

Did Mark Know This Proposed Narrative?

Mark's account of the Roman proceedings is shorter than John's. His two Pilate dialogues, one with Jesus and one with the Jews, are shorter than John's and missing a lot of what appears in John. Another major difference between Mark and John is that Mark directly dissociates Pilate from the Roman persecution of Jesus. In his version the whipping, mocking and abuse by the Roman soldiers takes place after Pilate orders the crucifixion and is no longer in Jesus' presence. In John, Pilate is a participant in the flogging, mockery and abuse. Mark also never has Pilate specifically declare Jesus innocent, while John has that happen three times. Does this mean that Mark did not know John's written source? Not necessarily. The reconstructed dialogue between Jesus and Pilate contains a number of matters that may have been offensive to Mark's theological perspective and he may have chosen to omit them.

The most significant portion of the reconstructed dialogue between Pilate and Jesus concerns Jesus' efforts to explain the nature of his kingdom and his prophetic role to Pilate. He talked of having a kingdom and he talked of God sending him into the world to speak the truth and how God controls Roman power. These public discussions about Jesus' true nature are inconsistent with Mark's theological viewpoint as expressed in his Gospel.

In Mark, unlike John, Jesus never explains the nature of his role in public. It is a secret. No human knows Jesus' true role. Not even Peter got it right. For Mark, the meaning of Jesus' life can only be understood by his death. Therefore, Mark wouldn't want to portray Jesus having discussions of his heavenly role with the Roman Governor. If Mark knew this source, I suspect that he would have removed all of the dialogue that had Jesus explain his role to Pilate.

A second problem for Mark, as with John, was the apparent rhetorical mistake made by Jesus in the response to Pilate's question about whether Jesus was King of the Jews. Mark couldn't allow Jesus to make a misstep. So, if he knew the source, I suspect that he simply truncated that portion of the dialogue showing Pilate one-upping Jesus.

If you remove Jesus' theological discussion with Pilate and truncate the portion of the dialogue where Pilate rebukes Jesus for his rhetorical mistake, you are pretty much left with nothing more than what Mark already sets forth, two simple questions and two responses.

A significant difference between John and Mark concerns the flogging, mockery and abuse of Jesus by the Roman guards. In John this takes place in between the two portions of dialogue with Jesus, and John makes Pilate a participant. In Mark it happens after Pilate hands Jesus over for crucifixion and Pilate has no role in the flogging and abuse. If Mark's goal were to disassociate Pilate, and thereby the Roman government, from any wrongdoing in the death of Jesus, then it would make sense for him to shift the brutal and cruel punishing scene to after Pilate is gone from the stage.

By eliminating most of the Pilate-Jesus dialogue and shifting the flogging, mockery and abuse to after the verdict, Mark has eliminated the need to have shifting locations during the dialogues, the way John has. Mark simply keeps Jesus in public the whole time.

Consistent with the exoneration of Pilate (and Rome), Mark may have believed that having Pilate declare Jesus innocent of wrongdoing and then showing him execute Jesus would create a bad impression of the Roman government. Condemning to death people declared to be innocent wouldn't exactly portray Roman government in the best light. Mark may have chosen to eliminate such a verdict so that he could emphasize the role of the Jews in pressuring Pilate to crucify Jesus.

One final major difference between John and Mark concerns who executed Jesus. We have already seen that both John and Luke use ambiguous language to imply that the Jews took Jesus and crucified him. If Luke used the same basic source that John did, this would suggest that the ambiguity was already in the text. However, Mark initially uses the same ambiguity. "So Pilate, wishing to satisfy the crowd, released Barabbas for them; and after flogging Jesus, he handed him over to be crucified" (Mark 15:15). But where John and Luke continue to use vague (but different) language to maintain the illusion of Jews executing the punishment, Mark follows up with an immediate indication that the Roman soldiers took Jesus (Mark 15:16). This was necessary in Mark's account because the Roman abuse takes place after the order to crucify Jesus. So Mark has eliminated what may have originally been an ambiguity in the written source. Mark was the earliest of the Gospels to be written and he may have well been aware that the Romans took Jesus and not the Jews. So he may have been attempting to correct an historical error in his source.

The discussion here shows that Mark could have known this written source and we have shown why Mark would have edited it in such a way that he John had such different versions of the Roman proceedings. But much of the argument here involves trying to explain the omission of details in Mark. This leaves open a reasonable possibility that the source used by John may have been written after Mark, and the details missing in Mark may have been added in at that later time. This is somewhat suggested by the fact that Matthew, written after Mark, doesn't seem to know this written source. If Luke knew it also, as seems the case, that would mean that if Mark knew it, Matthew would have been the only one of the four Gospel writers not to know it.

LUKE AND JOHN

Although I have noted above several of the parallels between John and Luke in the account of Jesus before Pilate, I would be remiss if I didn't touch on some of the ways that Luke differed from both John and Mark. Perhaps Luke's most significant departure from the other three Gospels in this episode is that Luke brings in Herod Antipas, ruler of Galilee, for part of the interrogation process. This introduces some twists into how Luke arranges events.

In John, Pilate expressed interest in where Jesus came from and asked him directly. In Luke, Pilate expressed a similar interest but asked the Jewish authorities if Jesus came from Galilee (Luke 23:6). Upon learning that Jesus did indeed come from Galilee he sent him off to be questioned by Herod Antipas (Luke 23:7). Luke and John have very different answers to the question of where Jesus came from. In John's version, Jesus remained silent; in my reconstructed version I proposed that he talked about his kingdom being from heaven. We have already seen that on occasion both John and Luke take significant liberties in reconstructing a story. So it is hard to be sure who comes closest to the original source. However, given that John's account suggests that he has re-arranged the previous written answers, I am inclined to think that John comes closer to the original source than Luke.

In Mark, Pilate asked two specific questions of Jesus; in John, Pilate asked several specific questions of Jesus. In Luke, Pilate asks Jesus only one question: "Are you the King of the Jews?" (Luke 23:3). Jesus responded with Mark's "You say so" (Luke 23:3). However, when Jesus appears before Herod we are told that Herod "questioned him at some length," but no specific questions are set forth (Luke 23:9). Luke says that Jesus remained silent when Herod questioned him (Luke 23:9).

This places Luke somewhere between Mark and John. Like Mark, we are provided with a very short specific interrogation by Pilate, and Jesus' only two noted responses are the same ones given in Mark; as in John, we are told that Jesus was subjected to a lengthy interrogation. It may be that, as I suggested in the discussion about Mark's relationship to the separate source, that Luke may have been offended by the nature of the discussion between Pilate and Jesus but that instead of deleting it he just indicated that some further unspecified dialogue occurred.

In John, Pilate has Jesus flogged and the Roman soldiers mock and abuse Jesus. In Luke, it is Herod's soldiers, not the Roman soldiers, who mock and abuse Jesus (Luke 23:11). When Jesus returns from Herod's interrogation Pilate twice offers to flog Jesus, but the whipping is never carried out (Luke 23:16, 22).

In John, when the soldiers mock Jesus, John makes no specific claim that Pilate is acting in a contemptuous manner towards Jesus. In Luke, we are clearly told that the mockery (by Herod's soldiers) signifies contempt for Jesus (Luke 23:10).

In both John and Luke there are three specific declarations that Jesus is not guilty of any wrongdoing, but on two of those occasions Luke adds to Pilate's verdict the additional comment that Jesus "has done nothing to deserve death" (Luke 23:15, with a slight variation at 23:22). In Luke, Pilate specifically suggests that the appropriate resolution of the case is to flog Jesus and release him. "I will therefore have him flogged and release him (Luke 23:16, 22)." John gives no specific explanation for why Pilate flogged Jesus.

In my reconstruction of the Pilate-Jesus dialogue from John, I proposed that the final statement in the original source was an accusation that Jesus claimed to be a king but that Pilate considered the claim to be ridiculous. With Luke's additional comment that Jesus has done nothing to deserve death, we can reasonably infer that Pilate thought that Jesus did something wrong but nothing to be taken seriously. That would reinforce the argument for my proposed reconstruction.

If we can assume that John copied from an earlier source and that Luke knew that source or a similar one, then Luke's departure's from Mark and John raise a couple of questions. The most significant is whether the Herod incident was original to the source used by John or due to Luke's own re-arrangement from some additional source or from his own imagination. If we accept that Mark also used John's source, should we accept that both Mark and John both omitted Herod's direct involvement while Luke retained it? Given our present state of knowledge about Gospel sources we can't answer these questions with any certainty. Luke's introduction of Herod into the process is the subject of much discussion and conflict in scholarly circles.

Luke has also provided us with a couple of other additional details not in Mark and John. He said that the mockery indicated contempt for

Jesus and that Pilate hedged his verdict by saying that Jesus did nothing *deserving of death*, implying that Jesus did do something wrong but nothing to bring on such a severe punishment. Luke also has Pilate says that the appropriate punishment is to flog Jesus and let him go. These additions of Luke support my reconstruction of Pilate's two dialogues in John. If I am correct then we have to ask if John deliberately omitted those references or Luke added them in. I am inclined to believe that Luke is closer to the original source in this regard

SUMMARY

In this chapter we looked at some apparent anomalies in John's longer versions of Pilate's dialogue with Jesus and Pilate's dialogue with the Jews. Our analysis suggested that some of the questions seemed out of chronological order and that some of the answers may have been switched around and assigned to different questions. This led me to see if there was a more logical arrangement of the questions and answers that eliminated the chronological disparities and offered a smoother narrative flow.

I have proposed a reconstruction of both dialogues that I believe solves these problems. If I am correct, then we have to assume that John must have had a written source and that he made changes to that source in order to portray events in a manner that reflected his own personal perspective about Jesus and the Jewish involvement in Jesus' death. I set forth a few examples of why I think John made such changes.

We then looked at the possibility that Mark may have also known this source and explored some of the reasons why Mark's personal viewpoint might lead him to omit so much material from the written source. However, since we were building the argument around material that was missing from the source we had to consider the possibility that the source post-dated Mark and may have been written to cope with deficiencies in Mark's version of events.

Lastly, we looked at some of the ways that Luke varied from both Mark and John. The most significant variation concerned the introduction of Herod into the interrogation process. This raised a question as to whether Herod's involvement was part of the original source material and John (and perhaps Mark) may have omitted it or whether Luke developed this narrative line in some other manner.

We also noted that Luke has a couple of additional details missing in both Mark and John which, in context, reinforce some of the arguments I made in support of my proposed reconstruction of Pilate's dialogues. These included the idea that Pilate held Jesus in contempt, thought his claim to being some sort of king was ridiculous, and thought that Jesus deserved a flogging but not a death sentence.

CHAPTER 5

The Gospels
as They Were Written
versus the Gospels
as They Have
Been Received

$\mathcal{A}$t present we have no original copy of any of the Gospels, or any other book of the New Testament for that matter.[116] Our earliest evidence for any written portion of the Christian scriptures dates to somewhere between about 110–150 and consists of just a credit-card sized papyrus fragment containing John 18:31–34, 37–38.[117] For the rest of the second century we have only a handful of Gospel fragments.[118] All-in-all, however, from the second to seventeenth centuries, we have over 3000 handwritten Greek manuscripts that contain, in whole or part, the New Testament.[119] We also have over 2200 lectionaries containing handwritten portions of the New Testament in Greek.[120] In addition we have some ancient copies of early handwritten manuscripts that translate Greek copies of the New Testament into other languages, including Old Latin, Old Syriac, and Coptic.[121] We don't begin to see complete written copies of any of the Gospels until the fourth century.[122]

The problem we face is that with the exception of a handful of small fragments no two of those manuscripts are identical in the overlapping portions.[123] The variations number in the hundreds of thousands, more than all of the words in the New Testament.[124] To be sure, the vast majority of differences can be traced to copying errors and when these are accounted for we can reconstruct most of the underlying text that lay behind these many copies. But in several instances we can see that scribes made significant alterations to the text they were copying from. We know this because we have copies of manuscripts in which the texts preserving particular verses differ in significant ways that raise important questions about early Christian beliefs. The existence of such variants was well known even in ancient times and many of the early church fathers commented on the differences in the texts and made judgment calls about what they believed to be most reliable readings. But they didn't always agree with each other.

Given the inconsistencies in the texts how do we know which version of conflicting passages most likely derives from the original scriptural authors and which represents an important deviation from what the original author wrote? To this end scholars employ a number of critical tools. We'll look at some examples further below.

TEXTUAL FAMILIES

The most significant discovery is that in many cases these manuscripts can be subdivided into families based on a variety of characteristics associated within the manuscripts. In several instances the text in one or more family groups differs from other family groups in significant ways. This not only provides some clues as to what the original text may have been but also leads scholars to conclude that most of the more important variations can be traced back to scribal activity in the first three centuries of Christianity.[125]

In those early centuries differences of opinion existed among Christian thinkers and teachers about the nature of Jesus, the meaning of his message, and the nature of his birth and death. This led to aggressive feuding and cross-accusations of heresy by assorted Christian thinkers. Some Christians taught that Jesus was not a god but merely that he was born human and adopted by God as a son some time after his birth. This belief is called the Adoptionist viewpoint. Other Christians taught that Jesus only appeared to be human and was actually some sort of spirit who experienced no suffering at his crucifixion, which is referred to as the Docetic viewpoint. Other Christians taught that Jesus and Christ were two separate entities, the one human and the other spirit, and that the spirit entered into Jesus after his birth and departed from him at his death. This belief, prominent among the Gnostics, is called the Separationist viewpoint.

Among those Christians whose teachings came to be identified as orthodox Christianity, these views were heresies. In the course of these debates the proponents of these conflicting theologies would cite portions of the Gospels as evidence in support of their position and opponents would challenge those readings. It is in this intellectual ferment that proponents of these assorted positions, orthodox and non-orthodox, may have made changes to the Gospel text in order to undermine the opposing view. Those making the changes probably thought that they were simply either just clarifying a misunderstanding or ambiguity or correcting an error in transmission.

For our purposes, we only need to focus on four of the main text families, the ones that have been most influential on Church traditions and scholarly debates. These are the Alexandrian, Western, Caesarean, and Byzantine. In some cases later scribes were influenced by more than one family tradition. For example, the extremely important fourth century Codex Sinaiticus follows the Alexandrian tradition for the Gospels and Acts but the Western tradition for the rest of the New Testament.[126]

The Alexandrian Tradition

The Alexandrian tradition originated in Alexandria in Egypt, one of the most important and influential intellectual centers in the Roman Empire. By the end of the second century Alexandria served as an important center for Christian scholarship.[127] The scribes were considered quite skilled, with an excellent command of Greek, and a number of New Testament manuscripts had their origins in this city.[128] Text scholars consider the Alexandrian influences to be among our best witnesses to the early New Testament.[129]

Among the best representatives of the Alexandrian texts are the fourth century codices Sinaiticus (for the Gospels and Acts) and Vaticanus, along with two papyrus fragments known as P⁶⁶ and P⁷⁵, both of which date to about the end of the second century.[130] (Scholars use the designation "א" for Codex Sinaiticus and the designation "B" for the Codex Vaticanus.) P⁶⁶ contains most of John 1–14, with about 440 alterations placed between lines, over erasures, and in the margins.[131] Most of these corrections appear to be attempts by the scribe to correct his own errors while some seem to be the result of the scribe consulting a different source text.[132] P⁷⁵ contains almost all of the Gospel of Luke from 3:18 on and most of the first fifteen chapters of John.[133]

Ehrman notes that the striking similarity in the Alexandrian witnesses from the papyri to Codex Vaticanus shows how carefully the Alexandrian scribes worked.[134] But, he adds, over the course of time some corruption may have affected the transmissions of later copies and scholars distinguish between the early Alexandrian line represented by Codex Vaticanus and later variations from Vaticanus.[135]

The Western Texts

The Western texts were so-called because of a belief that they originated in the western regions such as Italy or Gaul or North Africa.[136] Subsequent discoveries showed that it was not confined to just the Western regions. Ehrman says that the Western texts demonstrate a "love of paraphrase, resulting in clearly secondary features of addition, omission, substitution, and 'improvement' of one kind or another."[137] Because the Western texts have been cited by Church fathers from the second and third centuries, scholars place the origin of this tradition somewhere in the second century.[138] The chief representative of the Western tradition is the fifth century Codex Bezae, which contains the Gospels in both Greek and Latin.[139] Scholars use the designation "D" to refer to this codex.

The Western texts often contain longer readings than in the other families.[140] Its rendition of Acts runs about ten percent longer than it does in the Alexandrian version.[141] But in several places they exhibit shorter readings than those in the Alexandrian manuscripts.[142] Scholars refer to these occasional shorter readings as the "western non-interpolations" and they play an important role in the debate over the wording of the original Gospels.[143]

In some instances the Western non-interpolations create what scholars consider a "more difficult reading." The concept behind a more difficult reading is that where two texts disagree with each other and one reads in accord with accepted orthodox tradition and the other undermines that reading, the one that undermines the meaning is considered the more difficult reading. In some instances, there is no comprehensible explanation for why a scribe would have chosen to create a more difficult reading out of an acceptable reading. In such instances the more difficult reading probably represents a better approximation of the original text, and the more comfortable reading may reflect an alteration to the difficult reading. This is not a hard and fast rule and serves only as a guidepost. It is still necessary to examine the internal and external evidence, language styles, and many other features that could lead to a judgment one way or the other. In the text examinations below we will look at cases of "western non-interpolation" and see instances where the shorter reading is preferred and instances where it is rejected.

Since the Western tradition appears to go back to the second or third century, prior to the fourth century Alexandrian texts of the Codices Vaticanus and Sinaiticus, some who favor the Western non-interpolation over the Alexandrian texts believe that a corruption must have entered into the Alexandrian tradition after the underlying text found its way into the Western tradition.

The Caesarean Texts

It is generally thought that the Caeasarean text originated in Egypt and was brought to Caesarea by Origen in the early third century.[144] Caesarea was the most important intellectual Christian center in Palestine at that time and from there the text spread eastward to Jerusalem and Georgia.[145] Brown places its development somewhere between the Alexandrian and

Western traditions.[146] A number of text critics believe that the author of the prototype Caesarean text followed the Alexandrian tradition as his primary source and adopted those Western readings that didn't seem too improbable.[147] After arriving in Caesarea and prior to its spread, the manuscript evidence suggests that the Caesarean text may have undergone some changes or corruptions, although some question whether the earlier forms of the text were actually Caesarean.[148]

The Byzantine Texts

The Byzantine texts play a major role in the history of New Testament manuscripts. Their origins are somewhat murky but many believe they go back to the works of Lucian of Antioch, a late second-early third century Christian writer who produced a recension—a critical, thoroughgoing revision of a text—of the New Testament.[149] Comfort describes Lucian's recension as a revision characterized by "smoothness of language, harmonization, and conflation of readings."[150] That Lucian's work was somewhat controversial even in his own time can be seen from the following criticism by Jerome (late fourth-early fifth century), in his preface to his Latin (i.e., Vulgate) edition of the Gospels.

> I pass over those manuscripts which are associated with the names of Lucian and Hesychius, and the authority of which is perversely maintained by a handful of disputatious persons. It is obvious that these writers could not amend anything in the Old Testament after the labours of the Seventy; and it was useless to correct the New, for versions of Scripture which already exist in the languages of many nations show that their additions are false.[151]

Whether or not the Byzantine tradition originated with Lucian, the text is thought to have originated in the Syrian city of Antioch around the beginning of the fourth century.[152] For this reason scholars sometimes refer to these manuscripts as reflecting the Syrian tradition. Shortly thereafter, with Emperor Constantine's desire to promote Christianity throughout the Roman Empire, it became necessary to create scriptures for distribution. Byzantium, Constantine's capitol, had a substantial scribal community and they set to work on creating copies of Christian scripture for other communities and used the Antioch text as its underlying model.

This created a "conflated text that smoothes out difficulties and harmonizes the differences."[153] Brown says that it is generally looked on as a late and secondary development.[154] By the sixth century the Byzantine texts became the dominant tradition in the Christian church.[155] The earliest and best extant evidence for the Byzantine text, at least for the Gospels, is the fifth century Codex Alexandrius (not to be confused with manuscripts in the Alexandrian family), which scholars designate with the letter "A."[156] The Byzantine text serves as the source material for the Textus Receptus, which in turn served as the source for the King James (or Authorized) Version.

THE TEXTUS RECEPTUS

As a result of the prominence of the Byzantine text in the Christian church the overwhelming majority of our textual witnesses reflect the Byzantine tradition. Because the Byzantine texts vastly outnumber the other manuscripts the term "Majority Text" came into use, meaning a Greek version of the New Testament based on the Byzantine tradition.

Beginning around 1450 Gutenberg and others began to produce machine-printed editions of the bible, but none of these earlier versions were in Greek. Around 1514 the first printed edition of the bible to contain the New Testament in Greek came out in Spain. Because of its use of Hebrew, Aramaic, Latin and Greek it came to be known as the Polyglot bible. Its more technical name was *Complutensium Polyglot*. It was never put into general circulation and its underlying sources for the Greek text for the New Testament are unknown.[157]

At about the same time the publisher Jonathan Froben approached Desiderius Erasmus, a prominent scholar fluent in Greek, about preparing a Greek edition of the New Testament. Erasmus agreed to take on the project and began a search for texts of the New Testament in Greek but couldn't find any Greek manuscript containing the entire text.[158] As a result he had to piece together a source text from several existing manuscripts. He relied mostly on two manuscripts that most scholars consider rather inferior versions of the Byzantine text.[159] He placed numerous corrections in the margins and between the lines.[160] Commenting on Erasmus' edition of the New Testament, Brown observes, "Ironically, the Latin Vulgate, translated 1,100 years before, was based on better Greek mss.; and the English translation from the Vulgate (Rheims NT) at times was more accurate."[161]

The printing began in 1515. The first edition contained hundreds of typographical errors.[162] A second edition came out within three years and that edition served as the source for Martin Luther's translation.[163] Erasmus ultimately published five editions in total, the fourth containing his definitive version of the Greek New Testament.[164]

A contemporary of Erasmus, the Parisian printer and publisher Robert Estienne, who came to be known by the Latinized name Stephanus, began to produce his own version of a Greek New Testament. He brought out four editions from 1546 to 1551.[165] His third edition was the first Greek New Testament to contain a critical apparatus noting variant readings from fourteen other Greek codices.[166] Stephanus's third edition closely corresponded to Erasmus's fourth and fifth editions.[167] Stephanus's fourth edition published in 1551 incorporated two Latin versions of the New Testament along with the Greek and introduced for the first time the concept of numbered verses.[168]

Shortly after the publication of Stephanus's fourth edition Theodore de Beza, Calvin's successor at the Geneva church, printed a version of the Greek New Testament that for all practical purposes reproduced Stephanus's fourth edition.[169] This publication achieved wide-spread popularity and played a key role as a source for the King James (or Authorized) Version of the New Testament.[170] In 1624, Beza's publication served as the source for another printing of the Greek New Testament by the brothers Bonaventure and Abraham Elziver.[171] In the preface to their second edition, which essentially reproduced Stephanus's Greek New Testament as it appeared in Beza's edition, they included the following words, which

Ehrman describes as little more than the equivalent of a jacket blurb: "[the Reader has] the text now received by all, in which we give nothing changed or corrupted."[172] From this declaration came the term Textus Receptus and this version of the Greek New Testament came to be revered in many religious circles as 'the only true text" of the New Testament.[173]

There is a tendency to refer to the Textus Receptus and the Majority Text (i.e., a text derived solely from the Byzantine tradition) as if they were one and the same. This is almost true but on some occasions the Textus Receptus makes use of non-Byzantine passages so it is not a pure version of a Majority Text.[174]

THE CHALLENGE TO THE TEXTUS RECEPTUS

The Textus Receptus had become the standard version of the Greek New Testament almost from its inception. But as scholars began to systematically examine the ancient manuscripts and discover previously unknown manuscripts text critics began to question the viability of the Textus Receptus as the best possible reconstruction of the original Greek New Testament.

One of the most important pioneers in this field was the late eighteenth century German scholar Johann Jakob Griesbach. Ehrman says that Griesbach "laid foundations for all subsequent work on the Greek text of the New Testament."[175] He began a systematic study of extant variations of the Greek manuscripts and began to pay careful attention to the quotation of scriptural passages in the early Church fathers. He also studied issues related to the transmission of the New Testament text in the early centuries of Christianity.

Griesbach ultimately divided the ancient manuscripts into three categories, Alexandrian, Western, and Byzantine.[176] He classified what scholars now consider the Caesarean family with the Alexandrian tradition.[177] He set forth a number of rules about how to perform textual criticism, among which was the proposition that shorter readings should be preferred to longer readings on the theory that scribes were likely to add text rather than omit it.[178] He also offered a number of suggestions as to when the longer readings should be preferred.[179] Griesbach was the first major scholar to publish versions of the Greek New Testament that significantly varied from the Textus Receptus.[180]

Following in Griesbach's tradition a number of scholars brought forth additional evidence and continued to develop a critical approach to recovering the underlying Greek text of the New Testament. One of the first important scholars to challenge the authority of the Textus Receptus was Karl Lachmann, who collected many variants. In 1831 he published an edition of the Greek New Testament in which he listed places where it varied from the Textus Receptus. Lachmann did not claim to be publishing a copy of the original Greek New Testament, though, but rather a version of the text that was prominent in the fourth century before the rise of the Byzantine text.[181] His efforts earned him significant derision from the old guard.

Westcott and Hort, two important text critics whom we will discuss in a moment, wrote about Lachmann:

> A new period began in 1831, when for the first time a text was constructed directly from the ancient documents without the intervention of any printed edition, and when the first systematic attempt was made to substitute scientific method for arbitrary choice in the discrimination of various readings.[182]

Another important pioneer in textual criticism was the nineteenth century scholar Lobegott Friedrich Constantin von Tischendorf. Ehrman says that this scholar sought out and published more ancient manuscripts and more critical editions of the Greek New Testament than any other scholar.[183] In his eighth edition of the Greek New Testament, considered by scholars to be his most important, he assembled all of the variants that he or his predecessors had found in manuscripts, versions and Church fathers. Tischendorf had been the one who discovered Codex Sinaiticus and some text critics have accused him of over-dependence on that manuscript.[184]

One of the landmarks of critical scholarship on the Greek New Testament appeared in 1881, from the British scholars Brooke Foss Westcott and Fenton John Anthony Hort. Their *New Testament in the Original*

Greek consists of two volumes, one containing the Greek text and the other containing a detailed analysis of all the critical issues they encountered and why they made the decisions they did, and what problems they couldn't resolve.

In their work they identify four principal types of texts, Syrian (i.e., Byzantine), Western, Alexandrian and Neutral.[185] The Neutral text, they claim, is the most free from corruption and best represented by the Codices Vaticanus and Sinaiticus.[186] They propose that unless a case can be made against a particular reading, the Codex Vaticanus should serve as the closest form to the original Greek text.[187] One category of exception to their general preference consists of the "Western non-interpolations," a term of their own invention. Intriguingly, the Wescott and Hort edition influenced the editors of the Revised King James Version.[188]

In modern times the most widely accepted critical edition of the New Testament in Greek is the Nestle-Almond *Novum Testamentum Graece*, 26th and 27th editions, usually abbreviated as NA^{26} or NA^{27}. The same text also is used by the United Bible Society's *Greek New Testament*, third and fourth editions, usually abbreviated as USB^3 and USB^4. The chief differences between the two publications have to do with punctuation and the nature of the critical apparatus attached to the text.[189] Most scholars today would probably consider NA^{27} and USB^4 to be the standard text of the New Testament in Greek.[190] This doesn't mean they think NA^{27} and USB^4 are identical to the original Greek texts of the New Testament but only that it comes as close to the original text as our evidence allows. Within that context you still get some scholars who disagree with one decision or another about what should or shouldn't be included in the reconstruction of the original Greek New Testament.

TRANSLATION VERSUS UNDERLYING TEXT

I think it is important here to emphasize that the historical survey above is about what underlying Greek text stands behind the New Testament, not how to translate the text. Before you can translate a text you have to determine what text to translate. Once you agree on the underlying text you can argue over what it means or how it should be translated. For example, some bibles try to stick to the exact meaning of the words, some bibles might try to update the language to reflect the modern vernacular, and some might use some other criteria. The NRSV, for example, has tried to eliminate what might be thought of as occasional sexist language by translating the text in a way that eliminates the distinction between male and female in situations where the sense of the underlying text remains the same.

Broadly speaking, the primary debate about the underlying text is whether to use the Textus Receptus (or some variation of the Majority text) or a critical version such as NA[27] or USB[4]. Most bibles rely on one or the other before they decide how to translate the text. Some bible editions may choose some parts from one tradition and different parts from the other tradition. But first the editors must choose which underlying Greek text to use and only then can they decide how they think it should be translated.

Which underlying text one chooses can have a significant impact on how we should understand Christian origins. In the balance of this chapter I plan to illustrate how the differences between the two approaches to the underlying Greek text can affect our understanding of what the original text of the Gospels may have been and what consequences may flow from that understanding.

In order to keep this presentation simple and easy to follow, I will use English translations of the two basic reconstructions of the underlying Greek text. For the traditional Textus Receptus text I will use the King James (KJV) translation. For an English representative of a critical scholarly text I will use the New Revised Standard Version (NRSV) translation.

How Did the Original Gospels End?

Most New Testament scholars believe that Mark 16:9–20, the last twelve verse of Mark, were not part of Mark's original Gospel and were added at a later date by a different author. Similarly, most scholars believe that

John 21, the final chapter of John, was also a late addition to that Gospel by a different author. More contentious, however, is the matter of Luke 24:51–53, the last three verses of that Gospel, which are the subject of substantial debate. Matthew's ending appears to be intact. In this section we will look at some of the controversial issues surrounding the endings to Mark, John and Luke.

The Ending of Mark

One of the more interesting and problematic issues in textual studies of the Gospels concerns the ending of the Gospel of Mark. While Mark 16:9–20 appears as the final passage in modern versions of Mark, editions based on scholarly studies note that there are questions about whether this ending belongs to the original Gospel of Mark. The majority view among scholars is that these verses were later additions.[191]

The break between Mark 16:8 and 16:9 comes at an intriguing point. In the earlier sequence of verses, three women, including Mary Magdalene, had come to the tomb of Jesus to pay their respects. When they arrived they saw that the stone that had blocked the entrance had been rolled away and that inside there was a young man in a white robe. The youth told the women that Jesus had been raised and was no longer there, and that they should go tell Peter and the disciples that Jesus will appear in Galilee and that they should go there to meet him. Mark 16:8 then says "So they went out and fled from the tomb, for terror and amazement had seized them; and they said nothing to anyone, for they were afraid."

If Mark 16:8 were the original ending, then that Gospel ends with no direct witness to the resurrection of Jesus, except for the hearsay account of the unidentified young man, no post-crucifixion appearance of Jesus to the Apostles and no notice to the Apostles by the witnesses to the empty tomb. All of this leaves open the interpretive possibility that the body of Jesus had been removed from the tomb and buried in a hidden location. In the other three Gospels, the women inform the Apostles about what they observed, and Jesus appears to the Apostles, making clear that there was some sort of resurrection. Mark 16:9–20 appears to address this short-coming.

According to Mark 16:9, Jesus "appeared first to Mary Magdalene, from whom he had cast out seven demons." Her identification here with the casting out of demons is, presumably, intended to remind the audience who this woman was but this description seems a little out of place. If the same author was responsible for Mark 16:1 and 16:9, why didn't he attach it to her when he first introduced her into the story just a few verses earlier at Mark 16:1? That would seem to be the most logical way to organize the story.

Another inconsistency occurs with Mark 16:8 and Mark 16:10. Mark 16:8 says, "So they went out and fled from the tomb, for terror and amazement had seized them; and they said nothing to anyone, for they were afraid." But Mark 16:10 says that Mary Magdalene informed the disciples that Jesus was alive and that she had seen him. Mark 16:10 seems to conflict with Mark 16:8, as to whether Mary Magdalene ever informed the disciples as to what she saw. Interestingly, both Matt 28:8 and Luke 24:8–10 omit Mark's claim that the fleeing women told no one and they go on to say that the women did tell the others what they witnessed.

Mark 16:9–20 does not appear in either of the fourth century codices Sinaiticus and Vaticanus, which most scholars consider to be among our most important and influential witnesses to the original text of the Gospels.[192] In addition, the passages are missing from several other early texts that translate the Greek into other languages.[193] Ehrman notes that a number of early church fathers appear to be unfamiliar with these additional verses, including Clement of Alexandria (late second century) and Origen (3rd century).[194] Jerome (late fourth century) wrote "almost all of the Greek copies do not have this concluding portion.)[195] Many other ancient sources copying this section, says Ehrman, raise questions concerning its authenticity.[196]

On the other hand, the longer ending does appear in a large number of ancient witnesses and was already known in the late second century, having been included in the *Diatessaron*, a harmonization of the four Gospels by Tatian.[197] Ehrman argues that a textual analysis of the longer ending suggests that it is a secondary addition to the Gospel.[198] Some of the language, he argues, does not appear to be Markan in character and the shift from verses 16:8 to 16:9 seems disjointed.[199]

Complicating the issue is the presence of at least two other ancient appendages to Mark 16:8. The best known, referred to as the shorter or intermediate ending, is present in several manuscripts dating to the seventh through ninth centuries and is also present in many manuscripts that contain the longer ending.[200] It reads "And all that had been commanded them they told briefly to those around Peter. And afterward Jesus himself sent out through them, from east to west, the sacred and imperishable proclamation of eternal salvation. The KJV omits this passage but the NRSV places it in brackets to indicate its questionable nature and inserts it between Mark 16:8 and 16:9.[201] Ehrman argues that the language of this shorter ending is clearly un-Markan in style and betrays the hand of a later Greek theologian.[202] It also conflicts with the claim in Mark 16:8 about the woman saying nothing about what happened.

The other possible ending appears to be an expansion of the longer ending that, according to Jerome, appeared in Greek copies of his day and at least one ancient manuscript, known as Codex W and dating to the fourth or fifth century, contains this addition to the longer ending.[203] It's a lengthy passage that appeared after Mark 16:14 and this, too, according to Ehrman, has a secondary sense of a later theological addition.[204]

Despite the rejection of all three alternative additions to Mark 16:8, most scholars seem uncomfortable with the idea that Mark ended his Gospel at 16:8 or at least that he intended to end his Gospel at 16:8. Ehrman contends that while the external and internal evidence shows that the Gospel as we have it ends with 16:8, he finds it hard to accept that Mark intended to end his Gospel with the announcement that the women were afraid.[205] He suggests that the grammar indicates that something more should have been present, that perhaps the sentence wasn't finished due to some interruption to his work, death being one option.[206] A number of scholars have argued that there must have been some additional text and that it has been lost to us for some reason.[207]

The Ending of John

Most New Testament scholars see John 20:30–31 as the logical and natural ending of the Gospel of John.[208] It reads, "Now Jesus did many other signs in the presence of his disciples, which are not written in this book. But these are written so that you may come to believe that Jesus is the Messiah, the Son of God, and that through believing you may have life in his name." Yet, another chapter follows after that.

This additional chapter involves a new appearance by Jesus to the disciples and some conversations with Jesus. It features a frustrated Peter being asked three times about his love for Jesus along with a warning to Peter about potential future problems with his faith. Finally, it seems to elevate the unidentified individual known in John as the Beloved Disciple to a special status, implying that the Beloved Disciple would remain (alive?) with Jesus until Jesus' return. If at the end of Chapter 20, we were told that other things were being omitted but that the account given appears to be sufficient to convince people about the nature of Jesus, why would the same author then turn around and start adding additional stories?

The final two verses of John, 21:24–25, say, "This is the disciple [i.e., the Beloved Disciple] who is testifying to these things and has written them, and we know that his testimony is true. But there are also many other things that Jesus did; if every one of them were written down, I suppose that the world itself could not contain the books that would be written."

The first part of the passage describes the Beloved Disciple as the alleged author of the preceding Gospel but talks about him in the third person, indicating that the author of this final passage is someone other than the Beloved Disciple. The latter part of the passage seems unnecessarily repetitive of the ending of John 20. Both endings say that there were a lot of things that Jesus did that weren't recorded in the preceding Gospel. But in John 20:31 we are told that what was written was for the purpose of having you believe in Jesus as the Messiah. The implication is that these stories were true. In John 21:24, the author seems somewhat hesitant about how credible the stories may seem and asserts that we know the stories are true because we got them from the Beloved Disciple and we know that he tells us the truth.

These inconsistencies lead most Johannine scholars to see the last chapter of John as the work of a separate author from the rest of John. Johannine scholars, according to Raymond Brown, see the Gospel as the work of two hands, one author who composed the body of the Gospel and a redactor who made additions to the Gospel.[209] While Chapter 21 is widely accepted as the work of the redactor, some scholars have also argued that the redactor's hand is also evident in other parts of the Gospel as well.[210] Many Johannine scholars also believe the Redactor added in the opening prologue to the Gospel, a passage that they believe to have originally been a hymn that circulated in the community.[211]

The Ending of Luke

A good example of the problems created by the "western non-interpolations" can be seen with respect to Luke 24:51–52, two of the last three verses in that Gospel, which ends at 24:53. The Western tradition has a shorter version of this passage than the other manuscript witnesses. For a long time the scholarly consensus supported the shorter reading as original.[212] With the release of NA[26], which includes the longer reading, that view has been largely abandoned.[213] The NRSV has also abandoned that view but does note that some ancient manuscripts lack the questioned passages.[214] Still, some still believe the shorter version of the text comes closest to the original Gospel ending.[215]

Let's take a closer look at the problem verses. I have highlighted the controversial passages in italics. "While he was blessing them, he withdrew from them *and was carried up into heaven*. And they *worshiped him, and* returned to Jerusalem with great joy; and they were continually in the temple blessing God" (Luke 24:51–53, NRSV). The two italicized passages are missing from the Western tradition and if removed from the text they present a radically different ending to Luke.[216] The first passage is not only missing in the Western Codex Bezae but also in the very important Alexandrian Codex Sinaiticus.[217] The redacted version has Jesus depart without ascending to heaven and does not indicate that he was worshipped by the apostles.

The problem here, suggests Ehrman, is not merely that the shorter passage presents a more difficult reading (often preferred as more likely to reflect the original text) but that the longer version generates a chronological conflict with Acts, Luke's sequel to his Gospel.[218] In his Gospel, according to the longer version of the passage, Jesus ascended to heaven on the same day as the discovery of the empty tomb. In Acts 1:1–2 Luke tells us that he has previously narrated (in his Gospel) all that has happened to Jesus from the beginning "until the day when he was taken up to heaven." Then, in Acts 1:3–11, he presents a second narration of Jesus' ascent to heaven. In this second account, the ascension takes place forty days later (Acts 1:3). It is difficult to reconcile these two narratives.[219] If he had already narrated in his Gospel everything that happened to Jesus up to his ascent to heaven, why did he add this second apparently contradictory account?

There are three options with regard to this conflict. Either Luke included the apparent inconsistencies in his two volumes and both ascensions are original to Luke and Acts; or a scribe in the Western tradition deleted the ascension passage from Luke in order to eliminate what seemed like a conflict; or a scribe familiar with Luke's description of an ascension in Acts thought he should add in an ascension at the end of Luke so that it would be consistent with the claim that Luke's Gospel narrated all that had already happened to Jesus.[220]

Ehrman has very tentatively suggested that the shorter version may better reflect the original language and that the longer version was added not to resolve possible conflicts but to show a bodily ascension in order to counter claims that Jesus was merely a spirit and not a human being.[221]

Did John Know About the Adulterous Woman? (John 7:53–8:11)

The story of Jesus and the adulterous woman, with its familiar KJV phrasing "He that is without sin among you, let him first cast a stone at her" (John 8:7), is one of the most popular and oft-cited passages in the Gospels. But was it a part of John's original Gospel or was it added in at a later date? It is missing in the best early Greek manuscripts.[222]

Oddly, no Church father referred to this story as a part of the Gospel of John for over a thousand years after the Gospel was first published, including several early Church fathers such as Origen, who commented on the Gospel verse by verse.[223] The first Greek writer to comment on it, according to Ehrman, is the thirteenth century scholar Euthymius Zigabenus, who says that accurate copies of the Gospels do not carry this passage.[224]

The earliest Greek manuscript to make mention of it is the fifth century Codex Bezae, the best representative of the expansionist Western tradition, along with several Old Latin texts.[225] But its location in the text seems to shift around, including one witness that placed the passage in the Gospel of Luke.[226] Its present location seems to interrupt the narrative flow.

In the story that immediately precedes it, Jesus is in Jerusalem and the chief priests and Pharisees had ordered the arrest of Jesus but the soldiers failed to do so. An argument broke out over Jesus' prophetic status between the chief priests and Nicodemus, a Pharisee who supported Jesus. Nicodemus challenged the actions of the priests and argued "Our law does not judge people without first giving them a hearing to find out what they are doing, does it?" (John 7:51). The priests responded to Nicodemus's argument in John 7:52, saying "no prophet is to arise from Galilee."

At this point one would expect a new argument from Nicodemus or some further narration about what happened. Instead, we get the intrusive passage in John 7:53–8:11, beginning with, "Then each of them went home, while Jesus went to the Mount of Olives." Then we have the story of the adulterous woman.

Immediately after the story of the adulterous woman, in John 8:12, we have another abrupt switch. "Again Jesus spoke to them, saying, "I am the light of the world. Whoever follows me will never walk in darkness but will have the light of life." No notice is given at this point of a change in scene or who "them" was. In the story of the adulterous woman everyone but Jesus had already left the location. In John 8:13, however, we learn that "them" is the Pharisees, who accuse Jesus of "testifying on your own behalf; your testimony is not valid." And, it is only in John 8:20 that we learn for the first time that this confrontation took place in the treasury of the temple and no one came to arrest Jesus. In other words, immediately after the adulterous woman story we have been abruptly transferred back to Jerusalem but the notice of location for some reason is delayed until the end of the story.

So, we have a situation in which prior to the story of the adulterous woman, Jesus is in Jerusalem and Nicodemus is arguing with the Jerusalem Pharisees and priests that Jesus is entitled to a hearing before any legal action is taken; immediately after the story Jesus is in Jerusalem arguing with the Pharisees and accused of improperly testifying on his own behalf but no arrest is made. If we eliminate the questionable 7:53–8:11, in which we are told that Jesus departed to the Mount of Olives (outside of Jerusalem), we seem to have a partial account of the hearing requested by Nicodemus in which Jesus subsequently appeared to defend his actions. This would explain why there is no indication of a change of scene at the beginning of John 8:12. We are still in the same place we were before the intrusion of the adulterous woman story. This suggests to me that this argument with Jesus is the culmination of the story line that began prior to the adulterous woman story, in which the soldiers failed to arrest Jesus and Nicodemus asked for a hearing. That Jesus wasn't arrested after the confrontation suggests that he may have been acquitted of any wrong-doing.

I suspect that the insertion of the adulterous woman story breaks what may have been a larger story into separate unconnected pieces. If that were the case then the insertion works to downplay the idea that Jesus had been hauled into a Jewish court proceeding, gave testimony, and received exoneration from a Jewish court prior to the Passion period. Such an outcome would be inconsistent with the larger anti-Jewish themes in the Gospels' Passion accounts.

THE BAPTISM I AM BAPTIZED WITH (MATT 20:22–23)

One issue in recovering the New Testament text is the problem of harmonization, the process of scribes altering a text such that it conforms to another text in order to eliminate any conflicts or misunderstandings that could arise from the source text. An example of such an occurrence may be evident with Matt 20:22–23. Our early manuscript witnesses provide alternative versions of those verses, one of which includes additional text inserted into the corresponding passage in the other. Comfort says that most contemporary scholars consider the expansion of Matt 20:22–23 to be spurious.[227]

The thrust of the problem is that the longer passage does not appear in any significant manuscripts in the non-Byzantine tradition.[228] Kurt Aland and Barbara Aland, in their *The Text of the New Testament* (2nd edition), write, "The impressive manuscript evidence against it needs no comment."[229] Consequently, many scholars believe that Byzantine scribes made changes to the original text in order to harmonize the passage with Mark 10:38–39, which tells of the same incident.[230] Some modern editions of the bible, such as the KJV, display the longer version of the text and some, such as NRSV, display the shorter version. To appreciate the difference between the two branches of Matthew let me set forth the translations from the NRSV and KJV versions. The controversial additions are in the KJV translation and I have italicized the text in question. I will follow those two translations with the parallel passage in Mark 10:38–39.

> But Jesus answered, "You do not know what you are asking. Are you able to drink the cup that I am about to drink?" They said to him, "We are able." He said to them, "You will indeed drink my cup, but to sit at my right hand and at my left, this is not mine to grant, but it is for those for whom it has been prepared by my Father." (Matt 20:22–23, NRSV)

> But Jesus answered and said, Ye know not what ye ask. Are ye able to drink of the cup that I shall drink of, *and to be baptized with the baptism that I am baptized with?* They say unto him, We are able. And he saith unto them, Ye shall drink indeed of my cup, *and be baptized with the baptism that I am baptized with:* but to sit on my right hand, and on my left, is not mine to give, but it shall be given to them for whom it is prepared of my Father. (Matt 20:22–23, KJV)

> But Jesus said to them, "You do not know what you are asking. Are you able to drink the cup that I drink, *or be baptized with the baptism that I*

am baptized with?" They replied, "We are able." Then Jesus said to them, "The cup that I drink you will drink; *and with the baptism with which I am baptized, you will be baptized* (Mark 10:38–39, NRSV).

If you compare the KJV version of Matt 20:22–23 with the Mark 10:38–39 parallel in the NRSV, one might think that this was simply another indication that Matthew used Mark as a source and copied from him, as per our discussion of the Synoptic Problem. But if you look at the NRSV of Matt 20:22–23 you see that the text differs significantly from the KJV translation in that the NRSV is missing the references to "baptism" in Jesus' remarks. Because the added text is missing from the important non-Byzantine manuscripts scholars tend to favor the shorter version as more likely to reflect the original version of Matthew. This would suggest that Matthew had some theological problems with Mark's longer version.

GREAT DROPS OF BLOOD (LUKE 22:43–44)

One of the most controversial debates concerning the later addition of text to a Gospel revolves around Luke 22:43–44.[231] The scene takes place while Jesus is praying on the Mount of Olives just immediately before he is placed under arrest. The controversial passage reads, "Then an angel from heaven appeared to him and gave him strength. In his anguish he prayed more earnestly, and his sweat became like great drops of blood falling down on the ground."

Early witnesses to Luke disagree as to whether this passage was part of the original Gospel, and there is no easy resolution of the problem. In terms of sheer numbers the majority of manuscript witnesses include the passage.[232] But it is missing from the earliest Greek manuscripts and from most of the witnesses in the Alexandrian tradition, including the works of the third century scholars Clement and Origen.[233]

Ehrman suggests that if we relied solely on the evidence of the best textual witnesses most critics would probably consider this passage secondary, but that we also have to consider the widespread distribution of the passage in many early Latin and Syriac manuscripts and the commentary of Church fathers who know of the passage, including the second century scholars Justin and Irenaeus.[234] The conflicting evidence suggests that whatever change took place, addition or omission, happened during the second century.[235]

One key devisive issue concerns the nature of the language used in the passage. How faithful is it to Luke's style and thematic content and if faithful how uniquely Lukan is the controversial material? Some argue that the language reflects Lukan style and tradition while others argue that while consistent with Luke it is not uniquely Lukan.[236] Some have argued that while the material has Lukan characteristics they are not formulated in Luke's style.[237]

Another problem is that some argue that this particular portrayal of the anguished Jesus sweating great drops of blood appears to be incongruous with Luke's portrayal of Jesus everywhere else in his Gospel, including his depiction of Jesus on the cross. Following up in that vein, Ehrman points out that Mark, a source for Luke, has a parallel scene but has no reference to the angel and bloody sweat.[238] Mark does say, though, that Jesus "began to be distressed and agitated" (Mark 14:33). Luke, however, omits that line from his own account. Mark's account of this scene also has other indication of Jesus' anguish, Ehrman continues, but Luke omits all of those phrasings, too.[239] Luke, therefore, has apparently gone out of his way to eliminate all of Mark's specific references to Jesus' anguish.[240] Why, then, Ehrman asks, would he add this passage portraying such an emotional state after omitting his source's various claims to just such a condition?[241]

Textual scholars remain divided as to which version of Luke is original. The NRSV places it in brackets to show that there is a question as to the legitimacy of the particular verses. If the passage was a later addition, a question arises as to why it would have been added and accepted as if it were original. One argument that has been made in this regard is that it was added to counter claims that Jesus wasn't truly human and that inserting the passage provided evidence that Jesus experienced true human emotions and behaviors.[242]

The Parents of Jesus (Luke 2:33, 43)

Early on after the death of Jesus many Christians argued that Jesus was born as a human and that God adopted him as a son after he was born. This view has been referred to as the Adoptionist tradition. The emerging orthodox teachings saw that view as heretical and countered it by downplaying the role of Joseph as Jesus' father. Aspects of this conflict appear to be reflected in possible alterations to Luke 2:33 and 2:43.

The early witnesses provide two versions of Luke 2:33. The NRSV follows one tradition, the KJV follows the other. Here are the two versions, with the controversial text in italics.

> And *Joseph and his mother* marvelled at those things which were spoken of him. (Luke 2:33, KJV)

> And *the child's father and mother* were amazed at what was being said about him. (Luke 2:33, NRSV)

Note the subtle but important difference between the two. In the NRSV translation, the parents aren't mentioned by name but Joseph is clearly identified as the child's father. The KJV translation identifies the mother of Jesus as a parent but mentions Joseph only by name and not as a parent. Thus, in KJV the role of Joseph as a father is downplayed.

The version of the text reflected in the NRSV could easily be seen as supporting the Adoptionist tradition, that Jesus was the ordinary human son of a human father and mother, and it is easy to see how a scribe opposed to the Adoptionist view might have been motivated to overcome that possibility by modifying the text slightly to undermine the heretical interpretation. Which version of the passage is more likely to be closer to the original and which faction may have made the change?

The majority of Greek texts and several Old Latin, Syriac, and Coptic manuscripts have the passage as preserved in the KJV and it appears in the large majority of the ancient manuscripts.[243] It found its way into the Byzantine tradition and is the version that appears in its progeny. However, the alternative version reflected in the NRSV not only appears in many of the early manuscripts, it also appears in the manuscripts that text scholars consider to be among the best and most reliable.[244]

As previously noted, where the ancient manuscripts have conflicting texts, scholars tend to prefer the more difficult reading over the convenient reading as more likely to be closer to the original text. This isn't a hard and fast rule and needs to be applied in the context of other evidentiary considerations. Here, where the more difficult reading is also supported with a presence in the superior manuscripts and the early readings, along with a motive to clarify a possible heretical view, scholars tend to accept the NRSV reading of Luke 2:33 as the more accurate and the KJV version as a deliberate corruption of the original text.[245] Ehrman, who says there is little doubt that the majority reading (KJV) is a corruption of the original, also suggests that the wide diffusion of the variant readings indicates that this alteration came about early in the manuscript development, at least by the third century and very possibly in the second century.[246]

A similar conflict among the texts takes place just a couple of verses later, at Luke 2:43. Again, the NRSV follows one tradition and the KJV the other. Here are the two passages with the key words emphasized in italics.

> And when they had fulfilled the days, as they returned, the child Jesus tarried behind in Jerusalem; and *Joseph and his mother* knew not of it. (Luke 2:43, KJV)

> When the festival was ended and they started to return, the boy Jesus stayed behind in Jerusalem, but *his parents* did not know it. (Luke 2:43, NRSV)

Again, one version doesn't name the parents but clearly refers to Jesus' human father as a parent while the other gives the father's name but only refers to the mother as a parent.

On the other hand, at Luke 2:48, despite the existence of similar variances in a number of the ancient manuscripts, the change wasn't as widely distributed as were the other two cases and didn't enter into the majority of texts the way the other two did. The Byzantine tradition that led to the KJV did not adopt the change with respect to that verse. Consequently, the KJV still incorporates a reference to Joseph as the father of Jesus.

> And when they saw him, they were amazed: and his mother said unto him, Son, why hast thou thus dealt with us? behold, thy father and I have sought thee sorrowing. (Luke 2:48, KJV)

You Are My Son . . . (Luke 3:22)

Above I noted that when two versions of a text significantly disagree scholars often give strong consideration to the version exhibiting the more difficult reading but that other considerations also have to come into play. Here I'll give an example in which the majority of scholars choose the less difficult passage while a minority still argues for the more difficult version. Our subject is Luke 3:22, which also has important bearings on the Adoptionist controversy.

In the accepted version of Luke 3:22, after Jesus is baptized, a voice comes from heaven and declares, "You are my Son, the Beloved; with you I am well pleased." This reading is in accord with Mark 1:11, one of Luke's sources. But in a number of ancient texts and sources, the voice cries out, "You are my son, today I have begotten you."[247] This version of the passage can be identified with the LXX version of Psalm 2:7. So both versions of the text have a good source pedigree.

This alternative version of Luke 3:22 would certainly have provided fodder for the Adoptionist viewpoint. It is also the more difficult reading, which is often preferred over the less difficult reading. Nevertheless, the majority of scholars reject the difficult alternative reading.[248] Let's briefly look at some of the arguments on both sides.

In support of the accepted reading and rejecting the difficult reading, Comfort points out that the accepted version has the earliest and most diverse documentary support, including a late second century papyrus fragment (known as P[4]) containing portions of Luke 1–6.[249] He also argues that the variant version is localized mostly into the Western readings.[250] He cites Augustine to the effect that this Church father knew both readings and that the variant was "not found in the more ancient manuscripts."[251]

Ehrman, on the other hand, argues for the alternative reading. He notes that it appears in the fifth century Codex Bezae (the chief witness to the Western tradition), which contains the entire New Testament in both Greek and Latin. He further argues that among the witnesses of the second and third centuries that comment on this passage it is virtually the only reading that survives.[252] He says that not only was it the reading of the ancestors to Codex Bezae and of the Old Latin version of Luke, it appears to be the text known to Justin, Clement of Alexandria, Origen, Methodius and the authors of *The Gospel of the Hebrews*, *Didascalia*, and the *Gospel According to the Ebionites*.[253] With the exception of one Papyrus fragment (i.e., P[4]), he says, the accepted version is unattested in the second and third centuries.[254] Then, beginning in the sixth century that early version almost completely disappears from the manuscripts and is replaced by the less problematic text that harmonizes with one of the Gospels.[255]

Comfort suggests that the author of Codex Bezae "noted for his creative editorialization" may have been influenced by the Adoptionist view and made the change to enhance that position.[256] It should also be noted that the Gospels of the Hebrews and the Ebionites promoted the Adoptionist point of view so it is not surprising that they should favor that alternative reading. Comfort also argues that the New Testament authors tended to use Psalm 2:7 exclusively in connection with Jesus' resurrection.[257] Nevertheless, he accepts that Luke may have been influenced by Psalm 2:7 with respect to the first part of the verse, which everybody accepts, but that he was influenced by Isaiah 42:1 for the second part of the verse, which text has messianic allusions to receiving the spirit of God.[258] But, if Luke was influenced by Psalm 2:7 for the first part of the passage, it could be reasonably argued that he wouldn't abandon it for the remaining portion of the verse.

The above should give you some sense of the nature of the disputes and the problems associated with figuring out which version of a text is more likely to be closest to the original author's words.

THE DOVE (MARK 1:10)

Another issue with the same baptismal scene occurs in the Gospel of Mark and this involves another debate over heresy. Many Christians, especially Gnostics, believed that Jesus and Christ were separate entities and that the Christ spirit entered into Jesus after he was born. In the accepted version of Mark 1:10, we are told that Jesus saw "the Spirit descending like a dove on him." The problem is that almost all text scholars believe that the passage originally read that the spirit entered "into" not "on" Jesus and this reading would have given significant ammunition to those who argued that Jesus and Christ were separate beings.[259]

This alternative reading is found in the earliest and best representatives of both the Alexandrian and Western traditions.[260] Consequently, Ehrman argues, it is almost impossible to make sense of the alternative reading if the accepted Byzantine tradition was the original reading.[261] But, he adds, if scribes for the emerging orthodox tradition wanted to challenge the "dual beings" argument they would have reason to have altered the text to undermine that view by rejecting the text that says the spirit entered "into" Jesus and saying that it only settled "on" Jesus.[262]

Complicating the issue somewhat is that both Matthew and Luke had used "on" rather than "into" prior to the change made in Mark.[263] This suggests that in trying to deal with Mark's problematic phrasing, later scribes harmonized Mark's text with Matthew and Luke. Some evidence suggests that even as revised not all scribes were comfortable with the passage as a sufficient rebuke to the Gnostics, who argued that Jesus was a material being and that Christ was a spiritual being. In several early copies of Matt 3:16, the Markan parallel, the text says that the spirit came "to" Jesus, without necessarily touching him.[264]

"Do this in remembrance of me" (Luke 22:19–21)

According to Ehrman, no textual problem in all of Luke-Acts has generated more critical debate than that over Luke 22:19–21.[265] The ancient witnesses have six different versions of this text, four of which have been widely rejected.[266] The remaining two can be divided into the short version and the long version. The short version is one of the Western non-interpolations and exists only in the Western witnesses.[267] The majority of scholars accept the longer version as original.[268]

What follows is the longer version, with the controversial passage highlighted in italics.

> Then he took a loaf of bread, and when he had given thanks, he broke it and gave it to them, saying, "This is my body, *which is given for you. Do this in remembrance of me." And he did the same with the cup after supper, saying, "This cup that is poured out for you is the new covenant in my blood.* But see, the one who betrays me is with me, and his hand is on the table. (Ehrman 1993, 198)

While the shorter version would be considered the more difficult reading, very few ancient sources preserve it. It appears only in a few examples of the Western tradition, although one of the witnesses is the chief Western manuscript Codex Bezae.[270] Given the small amount of evidence for this reading, it is routinely dismissed as a corruption of the original text. But not everyone accepts that conclusion.

Ehrman argues on behalf of the shorter version as the original. He contends that the language and themes expressed in the additional text are uncharacteristic of Lukan terminology and thematic viewpoints.[271] For example, the underlying Greek phrase translated as "for you," he says, appears twice in the disputed passage and nowhere else in all of Luke-Acts.[272] The Greek word translated as "remembrance" appears only in this passage and nowhere else in Luke-Acts.[273] Outside of this passage, he adds, Luke never refers to a "new covenant" or "in my blood." [274] This last point he finds odd if it was original to Luke. Why throughout Acts would he not refer back to it? [275] In all of Luke-Acts, he continues, outside of this contested passage, Luke never says that Jesus died "for you" or for "your sins." [276] Throughout Luke-Acts the author rejects the idea of Jesus' death as an "atonement" and goes out of his way to eliminate that idea when adapting a text from Mark. [277]

In Mark 14:22–25, the parallel version of the Lord's Supper that Luke had as a source, Jesus breaks the bread and hand it to the disciples, as in the short version, but does not have Jesus say "Do this in remembrance of me," which also parallels the shorter version. Mark does have the cup and a reference to a covenant, as in the long version, but he does not refer to it as the "new" covenant as Luke does.

On the other hand, Paul in 1 Cor 11:23–26, written before Mark or Luke, has language that closely tracks the expanded the version of Luke. It has both breaking bread and drinking from the cup along with the phrases "do this in remembrance of me," "for you," and "new covenant." Did Luke know Paul's version of the Last Supper? Traditionally, Luke was thought to be an associate of Paul, although the claim doesn't appear to be easily supported by the historical evidence. But even if not an associate he may have been well aware of Paul's assertion about the Eucharistic meal.

Given the emergence in both Mark and Paul of this doctrine about the cup of wine, the dying for others, and the covenant, the important question asked by Ehrman and other supporters of the short form is why the Western scribes would eliminate these references from Luke's text if the long text was original. It seems to them to be inexplicable.

SUMMARY

In this chapter we looked at how the examination of ancient copies of New Testament manuscripts and the comments of early Church fathers about the existence of variations led to challenges to the Textus Receptus as the most reliable reconstruction of the New Testament available, particularly with regard to the claim of many religious figures that this is the only true text of the Christian scriptures.

We saw that in the first few centuries of Christianity manuscript copies of the Gospels and other New Testament books went through assorted changes and different editions of these books circulated in different communities at different times. Based on a variety of characteristics, text scholars divided these manuscripts into text families, the chief ones being the Alexandrian, Western, Caesarean and Byzantine families.

The Alexandrian texts appear to be the best witnesses to the text of the original Greek editions of the Gospels and other New Testament books, but not perfect witnesses. The Alexandrian texts contain a number of important variations from the Textus Receptus. For example, they do not contain the last twelve verses of the Gospel of Mark (16:9–20).

The Western texts were noted for the expansionist and creative editing of the New Testament books but on occasion they contained shorter readings than the Alexandrian manuscripts and this raised some important questions as to what the original text may have been. In some instances these shorter passages led to difficult readings and these raised questions as to whether these particular shorter readings were a better witness to the original Greek text of the New Testament than the Alexandrian and other witnesses that had longer readings. We saw examples of these problems with regard to the ending of Luke (24:51–53), where the majority opinion has shifted around, and with Luke's account of the Eucharist ceremony (22:19–21).

The Byzantine texts emerged during the fourth century and became the manuscript model for the Roman Empire, receiving wide distribution and becoming the dominant manuscript form in the transmission of the New Testament text in Greek. Text scholars, however, overwhelmingly believe that the source text for the Byzantine tradition was not a straight copy of earlier manuscripts but rather a recension, i.e., a deliberately created conflated text that smoothed out difficulties and harmonized differences to eliminate apparent inconsistencies. We saw one example of harmonization with regard to Matt 20:22–23, which exists only in Byzantine manuscripts and which scholars almost unanimously consider to be spurious.

The Byzantine texts served as the source material for the Textus Receptus. But the person who created one of the predecessors to the Textus Receptus, Desiderius Erasmus, had no complete copies of the manuscripts in Greek and pieced it together from incomplete manuscripts that constituted inferior versions of the Byzantine tradition.

Starting in the eighteenth century a number of scholars began to uncover new copies of the ancient manuscripts and began to collect textual variants and sort them out. A number of scholars, including Griesbach, Lachmann, Tishendorf, and Westcott and Hort, challenged the Textus Receptus by publishing alternative versions of the Greek New Testament based on the early manuscripts and assorted variants.

Today we have two broad standards being proposed for the original Greek text of the New Testament. In religious circles, the Textus Receptus still remains the accepted version of the text. In scholarly circles, the standard text is either NA[27] or UBS[4], both of which have the same underlying Greek text but differ in the nature of the critical apparatus offered and on punctuation issues.

CHAPTER 6

So, Who Wrote the Gospels?

*I*n the preceding chapters we explored various issues concerning the authorship of the Gospels and why New Testament scholars challenge the traditional claims that the authors of Matthew and John were two of the twelve Apostles, that the author of Luke was a traveling companion of Paul, and that author of Mark was a secretary to the Apostle Peter. The general consensus is that none of these authors were Apostles or closely associated with any of the Apostles, that the Gospels were originally written in Greek, outside of Roman Israel, and most likely written sometime after the destruction of the Jewish temple in 70 c.e. Although we don't know the identity of the authors we can say something about their backgrounds based on clues in their writings.

ABOUT THE AUTHOR OF MARK

The evidence shows that Mark was the first of the four Gospels to be written. This makes it difficult to determine how much of the Gospel was due to the author's own creative genius and how much depended on the significant use of earlier written sources. Given that Matthew and Luke incorporated about eighty percent of Mark into their own respective Gospels, it seems unlikely that there may have been a major written source that preceded Mark and upon which Mark relied but was unknown to these two other authors. It is possible, although still somewhat speculative, that there might have been an earlier version of Mark that had some differences from the received version and that this earlier version may have been the one Matthew and Luke knew about. That could explain some of the few minor occasions where Matthew and Luke agree against Mark.

On the other hand, in Chapter 3, we did a comparison between John 5–6 and a set of corresponding stories in Mark and saw a high degree of sequential alignment. Although we didn't have a lot of verbal agreement we saw that there were similar thematic expressions in both sets of stories. This suggested that either John knew Mark or that both knew a similar written source. It was also possible that the results were based on a collection of oral and written traditions and that the alignments were a coincidence. Johannine scholars are split down the middle as to whether John knew Mark. It was my own suggestion that John and Mark probably shared a common written source and each made modifications for their own literary purposes. Even if there were such a prior written source for Mark, it is hard to say how extensive it was beyond the areas already encompassed in our earlier discussion. That material makes up only a small amount of Mark's entire Gospel and to a large extent it seems that Mark brought together lots of independent stories from both oral and written sources and forged a truly unique document with consummate skill.

Mark wrote in Greek and on occasion in his Gospel he uses Aramaic terms that he has to translate for his audience.[278] This suggests that he was writing for an audience outside of Roman Israel where Aramaic was not the common language. Where this community was located is difficult to say and scholars have a number of theories.

Tradition, probably based on the unreliable evidence of Papias, places Mark in Rome and the tradition may be correct. We have some indications of a Roman setting for Mark's community. A number of scholars have pointed to a number of Latin terms and Greek loan-words from Latin in Mark's Gospel, suggesting he was influenced by a community where Latin was spoken.[279] This certainly hints at a Rome locale. Some scholars have also suggested that Mark 10:42, which refers to Roman oppression over the Gentiles, may have been an indirect reference to persecution of Christians. If this is the case it may be an indication that Mark's community may have suffered persecution. Outside of Roman Israel, at a time prior to the production of Mark's Gospel, the most likely place for such oppression would have been in Rome under Nero (c. 68–70 C.E.).

An interesting question about the authors of the various Gospels is whether or not they were Jewish. In Mark's case, the answer seems to be that Mark places Jesus in a Jewish framework but that Mark himself may not have been Jewish. The opening line of Mark's Gospel reads: "The beginning of the good news of Jesus Christ, the Son of God." The name "Christ" is a Greek translation of the Hebrew word "masiah" (or "messiah" as it is usually written in English), which means "anointed." As a title it means "the anointed one." Such an expression would have little meaning in the gentile world but in the Jewish community it was a term of great significance.[280] For Mark, then, Jesus is the "Jewish" messiah. But was Mark or his intended audience Jewish?

Perhaps the most important piece of evidence in this regard is Mark 7:3–4. "For the Pharisees, *and all the Jews*, do not eat unless they thoroughly wash their hands, thus observing the tradition of the elders; and they do not eat anything from the market unless they wash it; and there are also many other traditions that they observe, the washing of cups, pots, and bronze kettles" (emphasis added).

First, if Mark has to explain the nature of Jewish purity to his audience, it is likely that it is not Jewish. Second, Mark has made an error in explaining the custom of washing hands before eating by saying it applied to *all the Jews*. While it may have been a Pharisee practice, it was not at that time the practice of Jews in general.[281] This last point leads many scholars to question whether Mark was Jewish. In that regard, in our earlier analysis of Mark's opening sequence of stories I noted that in Mark 1:21–34 that the author appeared to be indifferent to certain Sabbath activities that may have been illegal.

While Mark places Jesus in the context of a Jewish messiah, Mark's understanding of the term seems to have gone through an evolution. A chief theme in Mark's Gospel is that no living human ever truly understood the true nature of Jesus until after he died. The most significant evidence in this regard occurs in Mark 8:27–33. It tells of the conversation between Jesus and the disciples over how Jesus is perceived. Peter clearly thinks of Jesus in terms of an earthly king, the traditional Jewish messianic view, and Jesus criticizes him for such an understanding.

Mark's messianic Jesus, he tells us, must suffer, be killed and rise up after three days, a concept alien to Jewish tradition.

In summary, Mark wrote in Greek for an audience unfamiliar with Aramaic. His audience appears to have been a gentile community unfamiliar with Jewish traditions. The community may have been Rome and it may have suffered persecution under Nero. Mark himself may not have been Jewish but he places Jesus in a Jewish messianic setting. However, his understanding of the Jewish messiah diverged from Jewish traditions.

ABOUT THE AUTHOR OF MATTHEW

The author of Matthew appears to be a reasonably well educated man capable of writing in a fairly sophisticated Greek. His Gospel also suggests that he was not only familiar with the Septuagint Greek translation of Jewish scripture but also with the Hebrew version.[282] Most scholars are convinced that the Gospel of Matthew was originally written in Greek and this suggests that he targeted a Greek audience.[283] Since the primary language of Jews in Roman Israel was Aramaic, a linguistic relative of Hebrew, scholars believe that Matthew must have produced his Gospel for a Greek-speaking audience outside of the Jewish homeland.

Approximately half of Matthew's Gospel depends on the Gospel of Mark as a source. Another twenty percent probably stems from a lost written source that scholars refer to as Q, although some scholars challenge this thesis. A large chunk of the remaining material encompasses his birth narrative. This leaves little outside of Mark and Q that tells us about Jesus' mission and last days. Matthew has functioned more as an editor than as an author. He has taken two or three large collections of writings and reshaped them to reflect his own concerns and theology. In that regard he has performed well. It seems highly unlikely, if the author of Matthew was one of the Apostles as Church tradition claims, that someone as creative as this author would rely so heavily on the wording of two other written sources from non-witnesses.

Matthew's Gospel contains a number of distinct features that provide us with some clues about the author's background. More than any other Gospel, for example, Matthew makes significant efforts to identify Jesus as a new Moses, i.e., an authoritative Jewish prophetic law-giver. Matthew's birth narrative clearly invokes the story of Moses' birth in the Book of Exodus. The Sermon on the Mount, where Jesus comments on the Ten Commandments and other legal principles certainly parallels Moses handing down the Ten Commandments and the law on Mount Sinai. There are also five major teaching discourses in Matthew, which many scholars see as a reflection of the Five Books of Moses.[284]

At the same time that he wrapped Jesus in a Mosaic mantel, he placed him in a direct line of descent from King David, marking him as the prophesied Messiah. This is significant in that some Jewish traditions held to a dual Messiah concept, one kingly and one priestly.[285] Matthew's Jesus combines both aspects, a priestly Messiah in the tradition of Moses and a kingly Messiah in the tradition of David.

Matthew also emphasizes adherence to Jewish law more than the other Gospels. "For truly I tell you, until heaven and earth pass away, not one letter, not one stroke of a letter, will pass from the law until all is accomplished. Therefore, whoever breaks one of the least of these commandments, and teaches others to do the same, will be called least in the kingdom of heaven; but whoever does them and teaches them will be called great in the kingdom of heaven" (Matt 5:18–19). In our examination of the Synoptic Problem in Chapter Two, we also saw that Matthew appeared to be deeply disturbed by Mark's indifference to two possible Sabbath violations by Jesus and reworked the material to eliminate any legal problems. This Gospel also depicts Jesus aiming his mission primarily at the Jews. "These twelve Jesus sent out with the following instructions: 'Go nowhere among the Gentiles, and enter no town of the Samaritans, but go rather to the lost sheep of the house of Israel'" (Matt 10:5–6).

These Jewish-themed elements strongly suggest to most scholars that the author of Matthew was probably Jewish and that he wrote his Gospel for a Jewish audience.[286] Evidence suggests that Matthew was especially popular with Christian Jews. One Christian-Jewish movement known as the Nazarenes adopted Matthew's Gospel as their own scripture and translated it into Aramaic around the end of the first or early second century.[287] However, they appear to have omitted the first two chapters of Matthew that discuss the story of his miraculous birth, as the Nazarenes believed that Jesus was born wholly human and that God chose him as a messenger because of his righteousness.[288]

On the other hand, there are also passages that reach out to gentiles. For example, "I tell you, many will come from east and west and will eat with Abraham and Isaac and Jacob in the kingdom of heaven" (Matt 8:11). This suggests that the Matthean audience also included non-Jews. For this reason, scholars believe that Matthew's Gospel probably originated in a city where Greek was widely spoken and that also hosted substantial Jewish and gentile populations. Since the earliest mentions of Matthew's Gospel appear in writings from Syria, most scholars would place the origins of this Gospel in the Syrian city of Antioch, which had large Jewish and gentile populations.[289]

One phenomenon that stands out in Matthew is the extraordinarily intense anti-Jewish polemics in his Gospel. In the scene where the Jewish High Priest interrogates Jesus, Matthew makes a significant change to Mark's account. Mark says the priests were looking for "testimony" (Mark 14:55) against Jesus. Matthew says they were looking for *"false testimony"* (Matt 26:59), a significantly more hostile charge than the one Mark makes. Matthew is also the only Gospel that depicts Pilate washing his hands of responsibility for Jesus' death and claims that the Jewish people as a whole called out, "His blood be on us and on our children!" (Matt 27:25). Given the very Jewish themes in his Gospel this degree of anti-Jewish polemic suggests to me that Matthew's Jewish community must have been heavily involved in conflicts with influential and important Jewish leaders.

In summary, Matthew was probably a Jew who wrote for a mostly Jewish audience, probably in Antioch. His community appears to have been in significant conflict with Jewish leaders in his home city. His Jesus reached out primarily to Jews and urged Jews to follow Jewish law. At the same time he saw Jesus as a fulfillment of messianic scriptural prophesy, uniting both the priestly Messiah and the kingly Messiah in a single person. He seems to have relied primarily on a couple of major written sources for almost all of his information about Jesus' mission and last days, which he creatively edited, altered, and integrated in order to promote his own point of view.

About the Author of Luke-Acts

It is difficult to draw much biographical information about the author of Luke-Acts based on the evidence available to us. Many of the theories put forth are subject to substantial debate. Scholars do agree, however, that he wrote in a polished Greek and had no direct connection to the inner circle of Jesus.[290] An important question is whether he had any connection to Paul, who was not a companion of Jesus.

A key problem in connecting Luke to Paul is that so much of what Luke says about Paul in Acts is inconsistent with what Paul himself says.[291] The author of Luke-Acts also exhibits no knowledge of any of Paul's letters and ignores many of the theological themes in those letters.[292] The chief argument in favor of a connection to Paul relies chiefly upon the so-called "we" passages, which scholars have thoroughly analyzed and argued over and which leaves most of them unconvinced. The consensus is that the connection to Paul was peripheral at best.[293]

Luke is the only Gospel author to acknowledge familiarity with a collection of prior sources but he doesn't tell us when he is working from a source and when he is using his own research and evidence. Approximately one-third of Luke is based on Mark and another twenty percent on either Q or Matthew. We also noted in Chapters Three and Four that Luke and John seem to share a substantial amount of information that suggests that the two authors knew a common written source for the Passion. Luke's Passion account suggests an attempt to harmonize Mark with this common source shared by John. This suggests at least two-thirds to three quarters of Luke derives from three written sources. If we eliminate Luke's lengthy birth narratives that leaves only a small amount of additional material in his

Gospel that is independent of these three written sources. Within that context, we see a great deal of creative effort in re-ordering, integrating and harmonizing of the source materials to create what he calls an "orderly" account of the life of Jesus. Indeed, the author practically boasts at the beginning of his Gospel that earlier sources exist but he needs to rework the evidence in order to create a more accurate history.

Luke seems to be the most scholarly of the four Gospel authors and appears to make significant efforts to cite precise historical details for context. For example, In Luke 3:1 he refers to John the Baptist starting his mission "In the fifteenth year of the reign of Emperor Tiberius, when Pontius Pilate was governor of Judea, and Herod was ruler of Galilee, and his brother Philip ruler of the region of Ituraea and Trachonitis, and Lysanias ruler of Abilene . . . ." At Luke 2:2 he tells us that when the Roman emperor ordered a Census at the time of Jesus' birth, Quirinius was Governor of Syria. In Acts 21:38 he notes that some Roman officials mistakenly thought that Paul might have been a Jewish revolutionary known as "The Egyptian." There are many such unusual historical details throughout his writings. Scholars generally consider him well-versed in the rhetorical conventions of Greek historians with some knowledge of Greek literature and thought.[294]

The author of Luke used the Septuagint Greek translation of the Jewish scriptures in his writings and appears quite familiar with the Jewish scriptural tradition.[295] This certainly suggests a strong interest in Jewish teachings and has led some scholars to argue that the author was Jewish. Other scholars vociferously reject that claim, and contend that he was a gentile convert to Christianity. They argue, for instance, that he misstates rules about Jewish purity in Luke 2:22. Brown has suggested that the best resolution of this dispute might be that Luke was a gentile who became a God-fearer, deeply interested in Judaism, and that he later became a Christian convert.[296]

The use of the Septuagint suggests that he probably was not from Roman Israel and lived elsewhere. This is reinforced by his dropping of all Aramaic expressions and names from his Markan source and substituting Greek variations.[297] He also appears to make geographical errors with regard to Roman Israel.[298] Some traditions dating to the late second century suggest that he was from Antioch and died in Boeotia but scholars debate the historical reliability of this claim.[299]

Luke-Acts is a Gospel meant primarily for gentiles and the author is clearly enamored of Paul, who claims to have been "entrusted with the gospel for the uncircumcised" (Gal 2:7). Thematically, he argues that salvation was initially offered through the Jews but Jewish rejection of Jesus led to its being offered into the Gentile world. An example of how he promotes this theme can be seen in the difference between his genealogy of Jesus and Matthew's. In Matthew, the author traces the family roots of Jesus from Abraham, the father of Judaism, through David and down to Joseph, Jesus' father (Matt 1:1–17). Along the way he traces the ancestry through David's kingly line of descendants. Matthew works down from Abraham to Jesus. Luke, on the other hand, works backwards, from Joseph back to the beginning of Creation, with "Adam, the son of God" (Luke 3:8). Luke, too, brings the line of descent through King David, but follows a non-kingly branch from David to arrive at the father of Jesus. The implication is that Jesus is, like Adam, a son of God, and his teaching is for all of humanity, not just the children of Abraham.

In summary, the author of Luke was probably a gentile who was drawn to Jewish religious teachings. He lived outside of Roman Israel and seemed well-versed in Greek rhetorical genres, with a strong interest in historical writing. He made substantial use of source materials and filled his work with many unusual facts that helped create a sense of time and place. He believed that Jewish rejection of Jesus required that the teaching of salvation had to be given to the Gentiles but that this was a form of continuity with Jewish law. Paul, the Apostle to the gentiles, seems to have been the most important religious figure in the author's world-view but much of what he writes about Paul seems inconsistent with or unaware of what Paul himself has to say.

About the Author of John

Identifying background material concerning the author of John is quite difficult and complicated by a lack of scholarly agreement on many questions. It is best here to just identify some of the questions in issue. What is widely accepted in Johannine scholarship is that the body of the work was written by one person, whom they routinely call the Evangelist, and that the final chapter, perhaps the opening chapter, and perhaps some other material came from the hand of a person commonly referred to as the Redactor. The Redactor may have made some editorial modifications to the body of the Gospel. The more complex issues are whether the Evangelist and the Beloved Disciple are one and the same and who is the Beloved Disciple?

Church tradition says that John, the son of Zebedee, one of the three chief leaders of the Christian community (along with James and Peter) after the death of Jesus, was the author of the Gospel of John and the Beloved Disciple. Raymond Brown, a leading Johannine scholar, observes, if John the son of Zebedee wrote the Gospel then he is almost surely the Beloved Disciple, but if he was the Beloved Disciple, it doesn't necessarily mean he wrote the Gospel.[300] Furthermore, there is no scholarly consensus that John, the son of Zebedee was the Beloved Disciple.[301] Many scholars believe that the Beloved Disciple, at most, was just a minor figure in the Jesus movement, but that he was highly revered figure in the community that produced the Gospel of John.[302]

In John 21:24, which most Johannine scholars attribute to the Redactor, the text says "This is the disciple who is testifying to these things *and has written them*, and we know that his testimony is true (emphasis added)." The implication is that the "disciple" is the Beloved Disciple. The question scholars ask is, what is meant by "and has written them." Did the Beloved Disciple wrote down all the preceding material or did he in the past write down some things that have been incorporated by the Evangelist?

Earlier, in the Gospel, when Jesus is on the cross and a soldier pierces his side and water and blood flow out, John 19:35 says "(He who saw this has testified so that you also may believe. His testimony is true, and he knows that he tells the truth.)" The incident described is presumably written by the Evangelist. The material in parenthesis—the parentheses are part of the translation and signify that the enclosed material is an observation by the author of the passage—could have been added by either the

Redactor or the Evangelist, but in either case, one gets the impression that the eyewitness mentioned is not the Beloved Disciple. Nor is the eyewitness identified. This would suggest to me that neither the Evangelist nor the Beloved Disciple was an eyewitness to the crucifixion.

Questions of identity aside, it is commonly thought among Johannine scholars that there was some sort of Johannine school of disciples, followers of the Beloved Disciple, whoever that might be, who kept his teachings and traditions alive.[303] The Evangelist and Redactor would both have been members of that community.

John 4 contains an extensive story about Jesus interacting with the Samaritans and bringing about several converts to his movement. This is in contrast to Matthew, who depicted Jesus instructing his disciples to avoid the Samaritans. This has suggested to many scholars that there may have been a Samaritan component to the Johannine community.[304] The Samaritans were a Jewish community that rejected Jerusalem-centered worship. They claimed descent from the northern Kingdom of Israel that was destroyed by the Assyrians in the eighth century B.C.E., Intense rivalry and conflict existed between the Jewish Jerusalem community and the Samaritan community (located between Jerusalem and Galilee.) Intriguingly, Pontius Pilate was removed from office on the complaint of the Samaritan legislature that the Roman Governor wrongfully murdered an important Samaritan prophet and massacred his followers.[305]

Elsewhere, John depicts Jews throwing followers of Jesus out of the synagogues. In John 9:22, for example, we are told, "His parents said this because they were afraid of the Jews; for the Jews had already agreed that anyone who confessed Jesus to be the Messiah would be put out of the synagogue." And, at John 16:2, Jesus says, "They will put you out of the synagogues." This has led a number of scholars to theorize that the Johannine community had experienced just such events. Implicit in this is that prior to the production of this Gospel the members of the Johannine community tried to worship within Jewish religious settings.

In summary, we can't say much about the background of the primary author of the Gospel of John. There is some evidence that the Gospel reflects the work of a religious school of followers of someone known as the Beloved Disciple. The Evangelist and the Redactor were both members of this scholarly community. It is possible that the Johannine community included converts from the Samaritans and experienced conflict when members tried to worship within a Jewish religious setting.

CONCLUSIONS

We have come to the end of our overview of the reasons why scholars reject the traditional Church teachings about the identities of the individuals who wrote the Gospels. I have tried to give you clear examples of why they draw these conclusions. In the preceding chapters we saw evidence for the following:

- In the first two centuries of Christianity the Church fathers had no clear idea who wrote the Gospels and began to speculate and guess. Their guesses became traditions and the traditions became accepted as fact.
- Mark was the first Gospel to be written and probably dates to after the fall of the Jerusalem temple in 70 C.E.
- Mark, Matthew and John appear to be unaware that the Jewish High Priest and his associates were Sadducees and active rivals of the Pharisees. In all four Gospels the Sadducee nature of the High Priest and his coterie goes unmentioned. Luke expresses some knowledge of this relationship in Acts but omits it from his Gospel. Such a lack of knowledge would be highly unlikely in anyone who was a close associate of Jesus.
- Matthew incorporated about eighty percent of Mark's Gospel into his own Gospel and Luke incorporated about sixty-five percent of Mark. This incorporated material amounts to about fifty percent of Matthew and thirty-five percent of Luke.
- Matthew and Luke each writing separately from the other, made use of a lost written source that scholars refer to as Q. This Q material amounts to about twenty percent of Matthew and Luke.

- If we separate out from Matthew the Mark, Q and birth narrative material, that Gospel has only a small amount of additional material about Jesus' mission and final days. This strongly suggests that Matthew was not an eyewitness to Jesus' missionary activities.
- Luke also seems to have shared a written source with John that contained a significant amount of material dealing with the Passion story. It is not clear how extensive that source was and how much use Luke and John made out of it.
- If we separate out from Luke the Mark, Q, the shared John source, and the birth narrative, there is not a significant amount of material left in Luke that treats the missionary period and final days of Jesus.
- Luke's frequent divergences from Paul's own claims about Paul's activities and his apparent lack of awareness of Paul's writings strongly suggest to many scholars that Luke's connection to Paul was tangential at best.
- Scholars are about evenly divided over whether or not John used Mark as a source. Our examination showed an extensive section of John that shared with Mark a high degree of sequential agreement and almost complete thematic agreement, but significant verbal divergence. My own suggestion was that Mark and John shared a common written source that they both altered for their own literary purposes.
- John appears to have had a primary author commonly called the Evangelist and secondary author commonly called the Redactor.
- As the Gospel texts were transmitted from scribe to scribe several changes to the original text were made. Some of these alterations or amendments found their way into the received version of the Gospel texts that came to be incorporated in the Textus Receptus, the Greek text that underlies the King James Version. These included such substantial additions as the last twelve verses of Mark, which significantly alters the ending of Mark, and the story of the adulterous woman in John, neither of which were part of the respective original Gospel. Several other small changes appear to have been made for a variety of

reasons, such as undermining heretical claims or harmonizing inconsistencies.

- The Textus Receptus, which underlies the King James Version of the New Testament, derives from the integration of several late edited copies of an ancient created text that sought to harmonize inconsistencies among various scriptural texts and smooth out problems. The authenticity of the original source texts was challenged by some early Church fathers.

- Modern scholars reject the Textus Receptus as the most accurate available reconstruction of the Greek text of the New Testament. The modern standard scholarly Greek texts for the New Testament is the Nestle-Almond Novum Testamentum Graece (26th and 27th editions, commonly abbreviated as NA[26] or NA[27]) or the United Bible Societies' Greek New Testament (3rd or 4th editions, commonly abbreviated as UBS[3] or UBS[4]), all of which utilize the same Greek text but which have different critical apparatuses and punctuation.

The evidence examined in the preceding chapters should give you a good sense of the issues scholars raise when examining the authorship of the Gospels and why they challenge Church traditions as to the identity of the authors. I emphasize that this work is only intended as an introductory overview and not an exhaustive treatment of the issues. I have included a bibliography in the back of the book and if you want to delve more deeply into these issues, the books included in the bibliography would be a good place to start.

Bibliography

Achtemeier, P. J. (1985), *Harper's Bible Dictionary*. San Francisco: Harper & Row.

Aland, K., Aland, B. (1995), *The Text of the New Testament: An Introduction to the Critical Editions and to the Theory and Practice of Modern Textual Criticism*. Grand Rapids, William B. Eerdmans Publishing Company.

Augustine, *De Cons. Evang.*

Bock, D. L. (2002), *Jesus According to Scripture: Restoring the Portrait from the Gospels*. Grand Rapids: Baker Academic.

Brown, R. E. (1993), *The Birth of the Messiah: A Commentary on the Infancy Narratives in the Gospels of Matthew and Luke*. New York: ARBL/Doubleday.

Brown, R. E. (1994a), *The Death of the Messiah: From Gethsemane to the Grave: A Commentary on the Passion Narratives in the Four Gospels*. (2 vols.) New York: Doubleday.

Brown, R. E. (1994b), *An Introduction to New Testament Christology*. New York: Paulist Press

Brown, R. E. (1996), *An Introduction to the New Testament*. New York: ARBL/Doubleday.

Brown, R. E. (2003), *An Introduction to the Gospel of John* (Francis J. Maloney, Editor). New York: ARBL/Doubleday.

Comfort, P. (2005), *Encountering the Manuscripts: An Introduction to New Testament Paleography and Textual Criticism*. Nashville: Broadman & Holman Publishers

Crossan, J. D. (1996), *Who Killed Jesus?: Exposing the Roots of Anti-Semitism in the Gospel Story of the Death of Jesus*. San Francisco: Harper Collins.

Ehrman, B. D. (1993), *The Orthodox Corruption of Scripture: The Effect of Early Christological Controversies on the Text of the New Testament*. New York: Oxford University Press.

Ehrman, B. D. (2000), *The New Testament: A Historical Introduction to the Early Christian Writings.* New York: Oxford University Press.

Ehrman, B. D. (2003a), *Lost Christianities: The Battle for Scripture and the Faiths We Never Knew.* New York, Oxford University Press

Ehrman, B. D. (2003b), *Lost Scriptures: Books That Did Not Make it into the New Testament.* Oxford: Oxford University Press.

Ehrman, B. D. (2005), *Misquoting Jesus.* San Francisco: Harper.

Ehrman, B. D. (2009), *Jesus, Interrupted.* New York: Harper.

Eusebius, *The History of the Church: From Christ to Constantine* (ed. G. A. Willamson, 1965) Harmondsworth: Dorset.

Fredriksen, P. (1999), *Jesus of Nazareth: King of the Jews.* New York: Vintage.

Freedman, D. N. (1996, c1992), *The Anchor Bible Dictionary* New York: Doubleday.

Freedman, D. N., Myers, A. C., & Beck, A. B. (2000), *Eerdmans Dictionary of the Bible.* Grand Rapids: W.B. Eerdmans

Frend, W. H. C. (1984), *The Rise of Christianity.* Philadelphia: Fortress.

Goodacre, M. (2002), *The Case Against Q.* Harrisburg: Trinity Press International.

Greenberg, G. (2007), *The Judas Brief: Who Really Killed Jesus?* New York: Continuum.

Jerome, *To Hebedia* (Epist. Cc.3)x

Justin Martyr, *Dial*

The Holy Bible: New Revised Standard Version. (1989. Nashville: Thomas Nelson Publishers. (Electronic edition from Logos Research System, Inc.)

The Holy Bible: King James Version. (1995)(electronic ed. of the 1769 edition of the 1611 Authorized Version.)Bellingham WA: Logos Research Systems, Inc.

Kloppenborg, J. S. (1999), *The Formation of Q: Trajectories in Ancient Wisdom Collections.* Harrisburg: Trinity Press International.

Liddel and Scott (1985, 1889), *An Intermediate Greek-English Lexicon Founded Upon the Seventh Edition of Liddel and Scott's Greek-English Lexicon.* Oxford: Oxford University Press.

Mack, B. L. 1989), *Who Wrote the New Testament? The Making of the Christian Myth*. San Francisco: Harper Collins.

Mack, B. L. (1993), *The Lost Gospel: The Book of Q and Christian Origins*. San Francisco: Harper Collins.

Mason, S. (1992). *Josephus and the New Testament*. Peabody, Mass.: Hendrickson Publishers.

Mays, J. L., Harper & Row, P., & Society of Biblical Literature. (1996, c1988). *Harper's Bible Commentary*. San Francisco: Harper & Row.

Meier, J. P. (1991), *A Marginal Jew: Rethinking the Historical Jesus: Vol. 1, The Roots of the Problem and the Person*. New York: ABRL/Doubleday.

Meier, J. P. (1994), *A Marginal Jew: Rethinking the Historical Jesus: Vol. 2, Mentor, Message, and Miracles*. New York: ABRL/Doubleday.

Meier, J. P. (2001), *A Marginal Jew: Rethinking the Historical Jesus: Vol. 3, Companions and Competitors*. New York: ABRL/Doubleday.

Metzger, B. M., Ehrman, B. D., (2005), *The Text of the New Testament*. New York, Oxford University Press.

Pagels, E. (1979), *The Gnostic Gospels*. New York: Vintage.

Patterson, S., Borg, M., Crossan, J. D. (1994), *The Search for Jesus: Modern Scholarship Looks at the Gospels*. Washington: Biblical Archaeology Society.

Roberts, A., Donaldson, J., & Coxe, A. C. (1997), *The Ante-Nicene Fathers: Translations of the Writings of the Fathers Down to A.D. 325*, 8 vols. Oak Harbor: Logos Research Systems.

Schaff, P. (1997a), *The Nicene and Post-Nicene Fathers* (First Series, 14 vols.) Oak Harbor: Logos Research Systems.

Schaff, P. (1997b). *The Nicene and Post-Nicene Fathers* (Second Series, 14 vols.) Oak Harbor: Logos Research Systems.

Vermes, G. (1981), *Jesus the Jew: A Historian's Reading of the Gospels*. Philadelphia: Fortress.

Endnotes

1 Brown 1994b, 109.
2 John 18:31–34, 37–38. Comfort dates the fragment to 110–125 (Comfort, 69.) Brown proposes a date of about 135 (Brown 1994b, 50.) Some scholars would date it to just the first half of the second century and others don't think that such a narrow time frame is sufficient (Metzger and Ehrman 2005, 56). In scholarly literature this fragment is categorized as P^{52}.
3 Comfort, 31.
4 Brown 1994b, 48.
5 Ibid.
6 Comfort, 91.
7 Aland, Chart 5A; Chart 6D–G.
8 Ehrman 1993, 27.
9 Ibid.
10 Mays, J. L., Mark 1:1.
11 Justin Martyr, *Dial*, CVI; ECF 1.1.6.3.0.106.
12 Eusebius, *Hist. eccl.*, 6:14, citing the writings of Clement who wrote around the end of the second century or early third century.
13 These include The *Gospel of Peter*, the *Gospel of Thomas*, the *Gospel of Mary*, the *Infancy Gospel of James*, the *Infancy Gospel of Thomas*, the *Gospel of Bartholomew*, the *Gospel of Matthias*, and the *Gospel of Judas*.
14 Brown 1994a, 1341.
15 Ehrman 2003a,15.
16 Ehrman 2003, 16.
17 See, for example, Ehrman, 2003b, 20, 32.
18 Crossan, 24, 26.
19 See, for example, Brown 1996, 5–7, 726, 749, and 762.
20 See, for example, Brown 1996, 5; Ehrman 2000, 262.
21 See, for example, Brown 1996, 5.
22 See, for example, Brown 1996, 5–7, 726, 749, and 762.
23 Eusebius, *Hist. eccl.*, 3.39.14–16.
24 Ibid., 3.39.13.
25 Ibid.,3.39.3
26 Ibid., 3.39.2
27 Ibid., 3.39.4
28 Ibid., 3.39.15.
29 Ibid., 3.39.16.
30 Brown 1996, 210.
31 Ehrman 2009, 287, ch 4 n 7.
32 Irenaeus, *Haer.* 3.2.1; ECF 1.1.7.1.3.2.
33 Eusebius, *Hist. eccl.*, 6:25.4–5.
34 Ibid.
35 Ibid.
36 Theophilus means God-lover.
37 See Acts 16:10–17, 20:5–15, 21:8–18, 27:1–28:16.
38 Brown 1996, 268.
39 Ibid., 324.
40 Ehrman 2000, 138.
41 Irenaeus, *Haer.* 3.2.1; ECF 1.1.7.1.3.2.
42 Anchor Bible Dictionary, sv."John, Gospel of."
43 See Brown 2003, 192–196 for some discussion of this issue.
44 These are the Codex Sinaiticus and Codex Vaticanus.
45 Brown 1994a, 4 n 1.
46 Ibid., 4 n 1.
47 Brown 1996, 162.
48 Ibid.
49 Ibid., 172.
50 Ibid., 226.
51 Ibid., 334.

52 Tim 4:11. Most New Testament
    scholars doubt that Paul wrote this
    letter (Brown 1996, 654).

53 Col 4:14. Most New Testament
    scholars doubt Paul wrote this let-
    ter (Brown 1996, 600).

54 Philem 24.

55 Brown 1996, 111.

56 Ibid.

57 Ibid.

58 Ibid.

59 Ibid., 117.

60 Kloppenborg, 72–73.

61 Brown 1996, 265.

62 Ehrman 2000, 77

63 Brown 1996, 114.

64 Ibid.

65 Ibid.

66 Goodacre, 1.

67 Ibid., 2.

68 Brown 1996, 114.

69 See the discussion in Goodacre,
    Chapter 8.

70 Brown 1996, 113.

71 Ibid., 112.

72 Ibid., 113.

73 Goodacre, 9–10.

74 Brown 1996, 113.

75 Ibid., 113–114.

76 Goodacre, 152.

77 Ehrman 2000, 77.

78 Ibid.

79 Although the Sermon on the
    Mount doesn't appear in Luke,
    much of the same teachings are
    present in Luke. See especially
    Luke 6. This shared language is
    part of the "Double Tradition."

80 Mark used the word *krabbaton;*
    Matt used the word *klinen* and
    Luke used *klinidion.*

81 Ehrman 2000, 77.

82 See, for example, Ehrman 2000, 77;
    Brown 1996, 114.

83 A variation on this parable also
    appears in the Gospel of Thomas, a
    collection of Jesus sayings that oc-
    casionally overlaps some Gospel
    material.

84 Brown 1996, 114.

85 Ehrman 2000, 79.

86 Ibid.

87 Ibid.

88 Kloppenborg, 51–64; See also
    Brown 1996, 117.

89 Kloppenborg, 80.

90 Ibid., 248.

91 Ibid.

92 Brown 1996, 122.

93 Brown 1996, 121; Kloppenborg,
    84–85.

94 Brown 2003, 95–8.

95 Ibid., 40.

96 Ibid., 58.

97 Ibid.

98 Ibid., 47.

99 Ibid.

100 Ibid., 48.

101 Ibid., 49.

102 Ibid., 103.

103 Ibid., 41.

104 300 denarii may have been well
    over a half-year's wages for a
    worker.

105 See, for example, Mark 8:30, where
    Peter identifies Jesus as the Mes-
    siah and Jesus orders him not to
    tell anyone.

106 Brown 2003, 100.

107 Ibid., 44.

108 Ibid.

109 Meier 1991, 225.

110 Ibid.

111 Mark 1:21 places Mark in a syna-
    gogue in Capernaum but doesn't
    say he lives there. Mark 2:1 says
    that he returned to Capernaum
    and indicates that he had a home

there. Matt 4:13 specifically says he moved to Capernaum.

112 John 9 has Jesus also heal a blind man on the Sabbath and receive death threats from the Jews.

113 Although the Synoptic Gospels all have a story about Jesus raising a young girl from the dead (Mark 5:21–43; Matt 9:18–26; Luke 8:40–56). Luke is the only Synoptic Gospel that has Jesus raise a man from the dead.

114 This creates some historical problems in that there was no doubt that Jews, as a general principle, could implement capital punishment. Early Christian commentators, noticing this lapse, correctly pointed out that under Jewish law they couldn't try anybody during a holiday period. But they failed to explain why the Jews couldn't wait until after the holidays to conduct a proceeding. We needn't resolve these problems here.

115 In my book *The Judas Brief* (Continuum 2007) I diagnose this entire scene in great detail and argue that the reference to "your King" was a teasing remark aimed at Jesus' followers and that Pilate never had any intention to release Jesus.

116 Brown 1996, 48.

117 Comfort, 69, dates the fragment to 110–125. Brown 1994b, 50, proposes a date of about 135. Metzger and Ehrman 2005, 56, indicates that some scholars would date it to just the first half of the second century and others don't think that such a narrow time frame is sufficient. In scholarly literature this fragment is categorized as P[52].

118 Comfort, 31.

119 Brown 1996, 48.

120 Ibid.

121 Comfort, 91.

122 Aland, Chart 5A;Chart 6D–G.

123 Ehrman 1993, 27.

124 Ibid.

125 Ibid., 28

126 Brown 1996, 50.

127 Ibid., 49.

128 Ibid.

129 Ibid., 50

130 Metzger and Ehrman 2005, 278.

131 Ibid., 57.

132 Ibid.

133 Comfort, 72.

134 Metzger and Ehrman 2005, 278.

135 Ibid.

136 Brown 1996, 49.

137 Metzger and Ehrman 2005, 308.

138 Ibid.

139 Ibid., 70

140 Brown 1996, 49.

141 Ibid.

142 Ibid.

143 Ibid.

144 Metzger and Ehrman 2005, 310.

145 Brown 1996, 49.

146 Ibid.

147 Metzger and Ehrman 2005, 310.

148 Ibid., 311.

149 Comfort, 97.

150 Ibid.

151 Schaff, P. (1997). *The Nicene and Post-Nicene Fathers Second Series Vol. VI.* Jerome: Letters and Select Works. (488). Oak Harbor: Logos Research Systems.

152 Brown 1996, 49.

153 Ibid.

154 Ibid.

155 Ibid.

156 Metzger and Ehrman 2005, 67.

157 Ibid., 139–40.

158 Ibid., 142.

159 Ibid., 143.

160 Ibid.
161 Brown 1996, 52.
162 Metzger and Ehrman 2005, 143.
163 Ibid., 145.
164 Ibid., 148.
165 Ibid., 149.
166 Ibid., 150.
167 Ibid.
168 Ibid.
169 Ibid.
170 Ibid., 151–2.
171 Ibid., 152.
172 Ibid.
173 Ibid.
174 Comfort, 98.
175 Metzger and Ehrman 2005, 165.
176 Ibid.
177 Ibid.
178 Ibid., 166.
179 Ibid.
180 Ibid., 167.
181 Ibid., 171.
182 Quotation taken from Metzger and Ehrman 2005, 173.
183 Metzger and Ehrman 2005, 172
184 Ibid., 173.
185 Ibid., 177.
186 Ibid., 179.
187 Ibid.
188 Ibid., 181.
189 Comfort, 101.
190 Ibid.
191 Brown 1996, 148.
192 Metzger and Ehrman 2005, 322.
193 Ibid.
194 Ibid.
195 Metzger and Ehrman 2005, citing *Epist. Cxx.3, To Hebedia.*
196 Metzger and Ehrman 2005, 322.
197 Ibid., 323.
198 Ibid.
199 Ibid., 325.
200 Ibid., 323.
201 *The Holy Bible: New Revised Standard Version*, 1989. (Mark 16:8).
Nashville: Thomas Nelson Publishers.
202 Metzger and Ehrman 2005, 325.
203 Ibid., 81, 323.
204 Ibid.
205 Ibid., 325.
206 Ibid., 326.
207 Brown 1996, 148.
208 Ibid., 366.
209 Ibid.
210 Ibid., 367.
211 Brown 2003, 84.
212 Comfort, 335.
213 Ibid.
214 See footnotes "p" and "q" in the NRSV text of Luke 24:51–53 as published in *The Holy Bible: New Revised Standard Version*, 1989. Nashville: Thomas Nelson Publishers.
215 Brown 1996, 274.
216 Ehrman 1993, 227.
217 Ibid.
218 Ibid.
219 Ibid.
220 Ibid., 228.
221 Ibid.
222 Metzger and Ehrman 2005, 319.
223 Ibid.
224 Ibid., 319–20.
225 Metzger and Ehrman 2005, 320.
226 Ibid.
227 Comfort, 329.
228 Ibid., 99, 329.
229 Aland, 307.
230 Ehrman 1993, 196.
231 Ibid., 187.
232 Ibid.
233 Ibid., 188.
234 Ibid.
235 Ibid.
236 Ibid., 188–9.
237 Ibid., 189.
238 Ibid.
239 Ibid.

240 Ibid.
241 Ibid.
242 Ibid., 188.
243 Ibid., 55.
244 Ibid.
245 Ehrman 1993, 55–6.
246 Ibid., 56.
247 Ibid., 62.
248 Ibid.
249 Comfort, 332.
250 Ibid.
251 Comfort, 332, citing *De Cons, Evang.* 2.14.
252 Ehrman 1993, 62.
253 Ibid.
254 Ibid.
255 Ibid.
256 Comfort, 332.
257 Ibid.
258 Ibid.
259 Ehrman 1993, 141.
260 Ibid.
261 Ibid.
262 Ibid.
263 Ibid.
264 Ibid.
265 Ibid., 197.
266 Ibid., 198.
267 Ibid.
268 Ibid.
269 Ibid.
270 Ibid.
271 Ibid., 199.
272 Ibid.
273 Ibid.
274 Ibid.

275 Ibid.
276 Ibid.
277 Ibid.
278 See, for example, Mark 3:17, 7:34, and 15:22–34.
279 Brown 1996, 161.
280 Ehrman 2000, 60.
281 Ibid., 74.
282 Brown 1996, 211.
283 Ibid., 210.
284 Ehrman 2000, 93. See Mark 5–7, 10, 13, 18, 23–27.
285 See, for example *Anchor Bible Dictionary, s.v.,* "Messiah", E.5 "Qumran scrolls."
286 Ehrman 2000, 101.
287 Ehrman 2003b, 9.
288 Ibid.
289 Brown 1996, 173.
290 Ibid., 268.
291 Ibid., 324.
292 Ibid.
293 Ibid., 326.
294 Ibid., 268.
295 Ibid.
296 Ibid.
297 Ibid., 265.
298 Ibid., 269.
299 Ibid., 267.
300 Brown 2003, 191.
301 Ibid.
302 Ibid.
303 Brown 2003, 196.
304 Ibid., 67.
305 Josephus, *Antiquities*, 18.85–88

Index

PEREJET PREJJ

If you enjoyed this book by Gary Greenberg be sure to look for this Pereset Press release

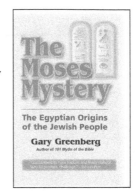

THE MOSES MYSTERY
The Egyptian Origins
of the Jewish People

The Egyptian Origins
of the Jewish People

Gary Greenberg
Author of 101 Myths of the Bible

What do history and archaeology *really* say about the origins of ancient Israel?

Although the bible says that Israel's formative history took place in ancient Egypt, biblical scholars and Egyptologists have steadfastly refused to explore the role of Egyptian history and literature on the origins of Jewish religion. *The Moses Mystery* attempts to set the record straight. Based on extensive research into biblical and Egyptian history, archaeology, literature and mythology Greenberg argues that the first Israelites were Egyptians, followers of the monotheistic teachings of Pharaoh Akhenaten.

Some of the many intriguing revelations in *The Moses Mystery* include:

- Ancient Egyptian records specifically identify Moses as Akhenaten's chief priest and describe the Exodus as the result of a civil war for control over the Egyptian throne

- Abraham, Isaac, and Jacob were characters from Egyptian mythology

- The Twelve Tribes of Israel never existed

An ingenious comparison of Biblical and Egyptian history.
—St. Louis Post-Dispatch

A must read for those interested in biblical scholarship.
—Tennessee Tribune

Insightful and valuable. —KMT magazine

Also by Gary Greenberg
101 Myths of the Bible: How Ancient Scribes Invented Biblical History
The Judas Brief: Who Really Killed Jesus?
Manetho: A Study in Egyptian Chronology

PEREƧET PREƧƧ

KING DAVID VERSUS ISRAEL:
How a Hebrew Tyrant Hated by the Israelites Became a Biblical Hero

In this controversial biography of one of the bible's most revered figures biblical historian Gary Greenberg challenges the conventional image of King David as a much beloved hero of the ancient Israelites. Originally published as *The Sins of King David: A New History*, the author has re-edited the manuscript, refined some of the arguments, and added many additional biblical citations.

I heartily recommend this substantial volume . . . [It] is a worthy addition to the library of first-rate and challenging books on [King] David. —Dr. David Noel Freedman, Editor of The Anchor Bible Dictionary and The Anchor Bible Project

---

Placing these texts into their historical, political, and geographic setting, Greenberg is able to separate much historical fact from biblical fiction. . .Greenberg shows David to be an ambitious mercenary, ruthless politician, unjust tyrant, and military imperialist. —Library Journal

---

Gary Greenberg will make you think. He might even make you angry. In his latest book he paints a portrait of a ruthless, deceitful, corrupt leader who was a traitor to Israel. —Green Bay Press-Gazette

---

Also by Gary Greenberg
**101 Myths of the Bible: How Ancient Scribes
    Invented Biblical History**
The Judas Brief: Who Really Killed Jesus?
Manetho: A Study in Egyptian Chronology

CPSIA information can be obtained
at www.ICGtesting.com
Printed in the USA
BVHW081918260321
603425BV00005B/614

9 780981 496634